The Alchemist

THE NEW MERMAIDS

General editor: Brian Gibbons
Professor of English Literature, University of Münster

THE NEW MERMAIDS

The Alchemist
All for Love
Arden of Faversham
The Atheist's Tragedy
Bartholmew Fair
The Beaux' Stratagem
The Broken Heart
Bussy D'Ambois
The Changeling
A Chaste Maid in Cheapside
The Country Wife
The Critic
The Devil's Law-Case
The Double-Dealer
Dr Faustus
The Duchess of Malfi
Eastward Ho!
Edward the Second
Epicoene *or* The Silent Woman
Every Man in His Humour
A Fair Quarrel
An Ideal Husband
The Importance of Being Earnest
The Jew of Malta
The Knight of the Burning Pestle
Lady Windermere's Fan
London Assurance
Love for Love
The Malcontent
The Man of Mode
Marriage A-la-Mode
A New Way to Pay Old Debts
The Plain Dealer
The Playboy of the Western World
The Provoked Wife
The Recruiting Officer
The Relapse
The Revenger's Tragedy
The Rivals
The Rover
The School for Scandal
She Stoops to Conquer
The Shoemaker's Holiday
The Spanish Tragedy
Tamburlaine
Three Late Medieval Morality Plays
 Mankind
 Everyman
 Mundus et Infans
Thyestes
'Tis Pity She's a Whore
Volpone
The Way of the World
The White Devil
The Witch
A Woman Killed with Kindness
A Woman of No Importance
Women Beware Women

The Alchemist

BEN JONSON

Edited by

ELIZABETH COOK

LONDON/A & C BLACK

NEW YORK/W W NORTON

Second edition 1991
Reprinted 1992, 1993, 1995
A & C Black (Publishers) Limited
35 Bedford Row, London WC1R 4JH
ISBN 0-7136-3071-X

First published in this form 1966 by Ernest Benn Limited
(edited by Douglas Brown and, following his death in 1964,
completed by Brian Morris and Philip Brockbank)

Published in the United States of America by
W. W. Norton & Company, Inc.
500 Fifth Avenue, New York, NY 10110
ISBN 0-393-90056-8

A CIP catalogue record for this book
is available from the British Library

Printed in Great Britain by
Whitstable Litho Printers Ltd.,
Whitstable, Kent

Printed in Great Britain by
Whitstable Litho Printers Ltd.,
Whitstable, Kent

CONTENTS

ACKNOWLEDGEMENTS

I have drawn gratefully on the work of many previous editors of Jonson's works and of *The Alchemist* in particular. Of the greatest resource have been the following works which I list chronologically:

John Upton, *Remarks on Three Plays of Benjamin Jonson, viz Volpone, Epicoene, and The Alchimist*, London, 1749

The Works of Ben Jonson, ed. William Gifford, 3 vols., London, 1816

The Alchemist, ed. C. M. Hathaway, New Haven, 1903

Ben Jonson, ed. C. H. Herford, P. & E. Simpson, 11 vols., Oxford, 1925–52

The Alchemist, ed. D. Brown, London, 1966

The Alchemist, ed. F. H. Mares, London, 1967

The Alchemist, ed. A. Kernan, New Haven, 1974

Ben Jonson, ed. Ian Donaldson, Oxford, 1985

ABBREVIATIONS

F	*The Works of Benjamin Jonson*, London, 1616
F2	*The Works of Benjamin Jonson*, London, 1640
H.&S.	*Ben Jonson*, ed. C. H. Herford, P. & E. Simpson, 11 vols., Oxford, 1925–52
OED	*The Oxford English Dictionary*
Q	*The Alchemist*, London, 1612
T.C.B.	*Theatrum Chemicum Britannicum*, ed. Elias Ashmole, London, 1652

INTRODUCTION

THE AUTHOR

BEN JONSON was born a Londoner in 1572, the posthumous son of an impoverished gentleman. His mother married a bricklayer shortly afterwards, and his circumstances in youth were decidedly straitened. Through the intervention of an outsider, however, he had some education at Westminster School under William Camden, who remained a lifelong friend; but he probably did not finish school and certainly did not go on, as most of his contemporaries there did, to Oxford or Cambridge. Instead he was apprenticed, probably in his stepfather's craft, about 1589, remaining in it long enough only to learn he 'could not endure' it. Before 1597 he had volunteered to serve in Flanders where, during a lull in the fighting, 'in the face of both the camps', he met and killed one of the enemy in single combat and returned from no-man's-land with his victim's weapons. The scene is an emblem for his life: the giant figure, a party to neither faction, warring alone in the classical manner before his awed onlookers.

Sometime in the early 1590s he married. By the time he was twenty-five he was playing the lead in Kyd's *Spanish Tragedy* for the theatrical manager and entrepreneur Philip Henslowe. As a writer he may also have composed additions to Kyd's work; he certainly did so for Nashe's satirical *Isle of Dogs*, and was imprisoned for the 'slandrous matter' in it. But already by 1598 Francis Meres listed him in *Palladis Tamia* amongst 'our best for tragedy' along with Kyd himself and Shakespeare. These tragedies, and indeed all the work of his early twenties, have vanished, but in the surviving records the man bursts upon the theatrical scene with characteristic and transforming energy.

In 1598 as well his first great success in comedy, *Every Man in his Humour*, was produced; in this, as in *Sejanus*, Shakespeare played a leading role. Within the same month Jonson killed an actor in Henslowe's company, Gabriel Spencer, in a duel. He pleaded guilty to a charge of felony and saved himself from the gallows only by claiming 'benefit of clergy', that is, by proving his literacy and hence immunity by reading 'neck-verse'. His goods – such as they may have been – were confiscated and he was branded on the thumb. His career was not yet fully under way: in writing of the incident, Henslowe refers to Jonson as a 'bricklayer'.

Still in the same year *The Case is Altered* was acted, once again with great success, and in 1599 or 1600 came *Every Man Out of his*

Humour, which – although it too enhanced his growing reputation – included in the targets of its satire the diction of some contemporary playwrights, notably John Marston. Marston may have annoyed his older friend by a bungled attempt to flatter him in *Histriomastix* a few months earlier, but he was in any case ready to take very unfriendly revenge for *Every Man Out* when, in late 1600, he caricatured Jonson in *Jack Drum's Entertainment*. Jonson countered with *Cynthia's Revels*, Marston with *What You Will*, Jonson with *Poetaster*, all in 1601. Thomas Dekker, previously Jonson's collaborator on the lost tragedy *Page of Plymouth*, came to Marston's aid with *Satiro-mastix*. But Jonson had gone beyond attacking his attackers: his plays, and particularly *Poetaster*, satirized influential men, and he barely escaped prosecution again. He withdrew, not yet thirty years old, from comedy and the popular stage, into the patronage and protection first of Sir Robert Townshend and later Esmé Stewart, Lord Aubigny, to whom he dedicated the fruit of his retirement, *Sejanus*.

Once again Jonson's talent for trouble caused him difficulty with the authorities, this time on the pretext of 'popery and treason' – he had become a Catholic during his imprisonment for killing Spencer – and once again powerful friends intervened to save him. Still again in 1604, when he collaborated with his reconciled friend Marston and with George Chapman on the comedy *Eastward Ho!* he was jailed, now for satirizing the Scots, for James I was king. But once more he was let off, and on the whole the accession of James I was of great benefit to Jonson: for this brilliant and learned court he wrote almost all his many masques, delicate confections of erudition and artistry in which he knew no master.

But it is to *Volpone* (1605), *Epicoene* (1609–10), *The Alchemist* (1610), *Bartholmew Fair* (1614) and *The Devil is an Ass* (1616) that we must turn for the central documents of his comic maturity, interrupted only by the tragic (and unsuccessful) *Catiline* of 1611. Jonson had by 1612 become conscious of the scope of his accomplishment, for in that year he began work on a collective edition which would enshrine in an impressive folio the authoritative text. His close connections with the court, doubtless enhanced when he gave up Catholicism about 1610, and the literary self-awareness begot by his huge reading in the classics, in part recorded in his common-place book *Timber*, led him, unique amongst the playwrights of his age, to take such pains with his *oeuvre*.

Jonson continued writing his masques and non-dramatic poems, but no stage play appeared after *The Devil is an Ass* until *The Staple of News* in 1625. Jonson's fortune declined in the nine years between. He began them with a walking tour of Scotland in 1618, where Drummond recorded their *Conversations*, and with a visit to

Oxford in 1619, where the University made him a Master of Arts. He ended them increasingly destitute of health, money and invention. His rule over the 'tribe' that met at the Mermaid was unweakened, but he depended more and more on pensions from Crown and City, especially when he failed to maintain with Charles I the favour he had found with the scholarly James I.

There followed *The New Inn* (1629), *The Magnetic Lady* (1632), and *The Tale of a Tub* (1633); the first was a disaster the last two did little to mitigate. Apart from a few verses he wrote nothing thereafter (his *English Grammar*, a draft of which perished in the fire that destroyed his library in 1623, probably goes back to a period as Professor of Rhetoric at Gresham College), although his lifelong habit of reading was not broken. He did not complete work on the second folio which was to include his writings since 1612. No child of his survived him, and it fell to his intellectual disciples, the 'Sons of Ben', to be his literary executors.

He died on 6 August 1637, at the age of sixty-five, and was buried in Westminster Abbey.

DATE AND SOURCES

The Alchemist was entered into the Stationers' Register on 3 October 1610. The earliest performance of which a record has been found was in Oxford in September 1610.[1] The King's Men, unable to play in London where the theatres had been closed since July on account of the plague, had gone on tour with *The Alchemist* and *Othello*. Some think it unlikely that Jonson would have premiered new work outside London and suggest that the play's first performance must have taken place earlier in 1610, before the company's exile in July. Without new evidence it is impossible to be sure but, since the play's whole fiction revolves around the situation of waiting for the plague to abate and taking advantage of the intervening time, it seems possible that the King's Men were doing perforce what many of today's companies choose to do – previewing their work in the provinces before a London run. Mammon promises 'to fright the plague/Out o' the kingdom, in three months'; Surly comments, 'And I'll/Be bound the players shall sing your praises, then,/Without their poets' (II.i.69–72). Perhaps poet Jonson scripted this in reference to his own players' impatience to get back within the city liberties.

If that were the case it would be in keeping with a play highly specific about the time and place of its setting, both of which nearly

[1] See Geoffrey Tillotson, '*Othello* and *The Alchemist* at Oxford in 1610', in *The Times Literary Supplement*, 20 July 1933, p. 494.

coincide with the circumstances of its early performances. The year is 1610 (the nineteen-year-old widow was born in 1591 [II.vi.31; IV.iv.29–30] and Ananaias confirms this date [V.v.105]). The date of the play's fictional setting is either 23 October or 1 November.[1]

The F text of the play lists the 'principall Comœdians' – the actors from the King's Men – who took part in the play's first performance. They are well-known names: Richard Burbage, John Lowin, John Hemminges, Henry Condel, William Ostler, William Eglestone, Robert Armin, Nicholas Tooley, Alexander Cooke, John Underwood. The King's Men had begun to use the theatre at Blackfriars as their winter house as an alternative to the Globe in 1609.[2] There is no external evidence as to which London theatre *The Alchemist* first played in but, given the play's fictional setting in Blackfriars (where Jonson also lived), it is very probable that Jonson anticipated using that theatre. He seems to have intended a great measure of coincidence between the circumstances of his fiction and those of an actual production in the date and location of his play.

There is no single source to the play though, as Alvin Kernan has pointed out, the plot is of a familiar farce type which involves the attempt to keep various individuals apart at all costs.[3] There is a loose parallel between the situation of *The Alchemist* and that of Plautus' *Mostellaria* in which a servant abuses his absent master's trust in a comparable way. Jonson would have known this as he would have known other literary treatments of bogus, profiteering alchemists, such as Erasmus' colloquy *De Alcumista* and Chaucer's *Canon's Yeoman's Tale*. But these works can in no sense be called 'sources.'

The play is, however, deeply informed by Jonson's extensive reading. '*Language* most shewes a man: speake that I may see thee'.[4] Jonson's belief that a man, as it were, speaks himself, to some extent relieved him of the burden of pastiche and he allows the occult and

[1] Ananias provides two possible dates in terms of his non-conformist calendar which makes March the first month (since, according to Puritans, this was the month of the Creation). In III.ii.131–2 Ananias estimates that in fifteen days time it will be 'the second day, of the third week,/In the ninth month' – i.e. 16 November, which gives 1 November as the date of the play's fiction. However, in V.v.101–5 Ananias gives the date on which the Brethren's pounds were 'told out' as 'the second day of the fourth week,/In the eighth month . . . The year, of the last patience of the Saints,/Six hundred and ten.' This translates as 23 October; but perhaps Ananias is referring to an event before the start of the play.

[2] E. K. Chambers, *The Elizabethan Stage*, 4 vols., Oxford, 1951 (repr.) vol. ii, pp. 509–10.

[3] *The Alchemist*, ed. Alvin Kernan, New Haven, 1974, p. 243.

[4] *H.&S.*, vol. viii, p. 625.

puritan writers from whose works he incorporates whole chunks to damn themselves with their own words. Dol, in her 'fit', recites passages from Hugh Broughton's *A Concent of Scripture*. Subtle's explanation of the alchemical process in II.iii. is taken – at times verbatim – from Martin Delrio's *Disquisitiones Magicae*. In *Volpone* the gentleman-traveller, Peregrine, agrees with Sir Politic that the mountebank's language is 'rare': 'But alchemy,/I never heard the like – or Broughton's books' (II.ii.118–19). In *The Alchemist* Jonson does not tamper with the rare languages of Broughton and alchemy – except to lift them out of any context where it is possible to take them seriously. *H.&S.* also record quotations from Arnold of Villa Nova's *Rosarium Philosophorum* (II.i.39, 40; II.iii.106–14), Geber's *Summa Perfectionis* (II.v.35–6), Paracelsus' *Manuale de Lapide Philosophico* (II.ii.25–8, II.v.28), and Robertus Vallensis' *De Veritate et Antiquitate Artis Chemicae* (II.i.101–4).

Jonson, whose plays are so full of the circumstantial reality of Jacobean life, incorporates current news into the play. Fifty years later Margaret of Newcastle was to develop the hypothesis that Jonson's satire was specifically directed at the Elizabethan occultist, John Dee, and his assistant, Edward Kelley, Dol and Dame Pliant representing their two, pooled, wives.[1] The play's satire is clearly wider than this suggestion allows but John Dee does appear in Abel Drugger's rebus and Jonson's knowledge of him and Kelley is part of the play's context. The gulling of the credulous Dapper by the Queen of Fairy had a contemporary parallel in the case of Thomas Rogers, a Dorset man of marriageable age, who was robbed of £6 by two brothers who promised him an introduction to the Fairy Queen who would then willingly be his bride. This case came to Chancery between November 1609 and February 1610.[2] The hint Jonson takes from this news item reflects his alertness to any material which could be of use.

ALCHEMY AND WIT

The Alchemist is often described as if it were a satire which exposed the fraudulence of alchemy – the process which transforms base metals into gold. In fact Jonson's play is neither exposure nor celebration of alchemy *per se*: Subtle and Face, the two central characters, though sufficiently learned in alchemical lore to awe their clients, are not alchemists but con men.

A true alchemist would, almost of necessity, be hard to identify. Successful alchemical projection was believed to require not only an

[1] ibid., vol. x, p. 47.
[2] ibid., vol. x, pp. 47–8.

absolutely meticulous attention to material requirements but also a rare spiritual purity of the practitioner. One might go so far as to say that the Philosopher's Stone, so avidly sought by the greedy, would only be granted to a person so free of self interest as not to want it. A person of such purity – without cupidity or material ambition – would hardly care to try whether they could indeed make material gold. Their goal would be an alchemy and regeneration of the spirit beside which the power to transmute metals would appear a negligible trick and not one to be advertised.[1]

Inevitably it was the charlatans and profiteers who were most in evidence, not those on the path to true alchemy. Nevertheless there were some who, while not successful, were not knowing frauds. They might themselves have attributed their failure to their lack of spiritual development, or to some error in the minutely demanding material process. Such may have been Cornelius de Lannoy whom Elizabeth I imprisoned when he failed to come up with the stone. He pleaded that 'if it shall please the Queen to release him from confinement he will without delay put into operation that wonderful elixir for making gold for her majesty's service'.[2]

Subtle speaks of being 'locked up, in the Tower, forever,/To make gold there (for th' state)' (IV.vii.81–2) and, though Elizabeth's patronage of learned occultists such as John Dee was not primarily from mercenary motives, alchemy was clearly seen as a means of replenishing state coffers. But such hopes misunderstood the nature of the Philosopher's Stone whose virtue (meaning both 'power' and 'goodness' and 'power through goodness') could never become a transferable commodity.

The virtue (power to do good) of the stone is both consequence and symbol of the virtue (powerful because good) of its possessor. Sir Epicure Mammon, the play's master consumer, does not grasp this. He believes that the stone is able to originate the virtue which it reflects and answers in its possessor. He believes that the stone 'by its virtue,/Can confer honour, love, respect, long life,/Give safety, valour: yea, and victory,/To whom he will' (II.i.49–52). Later Subtle cautions him that the man who will possess the stone must be '*homo frugi*,/A pious, holy, and religious man,/One free from mortal sin, a very virgin.' That, as Mammon sees it, is Subtle the 'alchemist's' business – 'That makes it, sir, he is so.' For himself he promises a shorter way, 'But I buy it' (II.ii.97–100).

[1] For more information on this more reputable alchemical tradition see Frances A. Yates, *The Rosicrucian Enlightenment*, London, 1972 (particularly chapter 14) and Allen G. Debus, *The English Paracelsians*, London, 1965.

[2] Quoted by Hathaway in the introduction to his edition of *The Alchemist*, New York, 1903, p. 37.

This more everyday alchemy – by which money is converted into commodity and stuff converted into revenue – is in evidence throughout the play. The first mention of the Philosopher's Stone is as a synonym for a source of profit:

> I will have
> A book, but barely reckoning thy impostures,
> Shall prove a true philosopher's stone, to printers.
> (I.i.101–2)

Alchemy also comes up in this first scene as a metaphor for social transformation. Subtle reminds Face of how he 'Sublimed [him], and exalted [him], and fixed [him]/I' the third region' (I.i.68–9). Subtle has 'translated' Face, and in turn the two of them find in the base matter of their fellow citizens a propensity to be converted into profit. When Face confronts Subtle with the claim that his contribution is indispensible, the 'stuff' he refers to is human stuff:

> You must have stuff, brought home to you, to work on?
> And, yet, you think, I am at no expense,
> In searching out these veins, then following 'em,
> Then trying 'em out. (I.iii.104–7)

These words are echoed by Mammon in the next act. But this time they refer to lead and iron:

> My only care is,
> Where to get stuff, enough now, to project on,
> This town will not half serve me. (II.ii.11–13)

The pretence of alchemy at the centre of the play's plot acts most powerfully as a metaphor and an example of the several kinds of transformation – social, linguistic and economic – which concern the play's personnel. The charade of alchemy acts as a kind of cartoon or emblem of this more generally diffused process.

But while Face and Subtle's highly informed pretence of alchemy is the play's central unifying metaphor, it is only one of their several means of transforming unpromising stuff into the means of personal gain. The city which Jonson portrays is populated by citizens on the make. The play reflects a period and an environment of rapid upward mobility in which landed wealth began to be superseded by wealth from other sources and the kind of 'modern happiness' by which a Dol Common could become a great lady was more available than before. This kind of social alchemy can be seen in such details as the kinds of utensils possessed by working people. In 1577 William Harrison recorded that, in his part of Essex, villagers had replaced their 'treen' (wooden) platters with pewter, and that instead of wooden spoons they now used implements made of silver or tin.[1] Such transformations were considerably more rapid in the city.

All the inhabitants of the play share a hunger for upward mobility: they want not just wealth, but its accoutrements. Face describes Subtle's wonderful powers in terms of the kind of credit his clients might reasonably come to expect:

> You shall have a cast commander, (can but get
> In credit with a glover, or a spurrier,
> For some two pair, of either's ware, aforehand)
> Will, by most swift posts, dealing with him,
> Arrive at competent means, to keep himself,
> His punk, and naked body, in excellent fashion.
> And be admired for it. (III.iv.76–82)

A credit limit which once extended only to the cost of two pairs of gloves will now stretch to stylish clothes for an entire household. But, significantly, this household does not comprise a nuclear family; the other occupants – the kept woman and the catamite – are also status commodities. This is the world which Jonson vilifies in his 'Epistle to a Friend to persuade him to the Wars' – a world in which bonds of affection have been replaced by acquisition and purchase and 'Adulteries . . . [are] grown commodities upon exchange.' In *The Alchemist* we see the nubile widow, Dame Pliant, being used as a transferable promissory note, offered in several extremities though only 'cashed in' by Lovewit at the end.

But though he recognised and castigated the moral depletion of the 'money get' age in which all is reduced to commodity, Jonson was clearly intrigued by the curious equivalences between stuffs that market valuations could create. The so-called 'commodity swindle' is mentioned twice in the play. This was the practice by which a money-lender would take advantage of his client in order to force him to accept part of the loan in unwanted commodities which he wished to offload – 'be it pepper, soap,/Hops, or tobacco, oatmeal, woad, or cheeses' (III.iv.97–8) – at inflated valuations.

The gulls – consumers to a man – reveal their imaginative scope in terms of their material ambitions, and it is revealing of the Puritans' pinched minds that what they want out of Subtle is, specifically, coin. All the others expect their investment to lead to some kind of transformation, but the Puritans just want more of the same. The only scope available to them is the minute room for play within the quibble between 'coining' and 'casting' (III.ii.151–2).

[1] William Harrison, *Description of England* (1577), ed. G. Edelen, New York, 1968, pp. 200–1.

Face likes coins as well as wealth. With their various heads they are emblems of himself. At the end of Act III scene iv he empties Dapper's purse in the name of obtaining gratuities for the Fairy Queen's retinue. Dapper hands over 'six score Edward shillings ... an old Harry's sovereign ... three James shillings, and an Elizabeth groat ..., Just twenty nobles'. Face urges more, 'I would you had the other noble in Marys.' Dapper has 'some Philip, and Marys'. 'Ay, those same/Are best of all', says Face. He is not simply greedy: he is an amateur numismatist taking pleasure in the individual particulars of coins and not just in their equivalent value. In this he recalls a character in a play written by Dekker ten years before *The Alchemist.* Firk, in *The Shoemaker's Holiday*, is given a threepenny bit which, for a moment, he thinks only three ha'pence till the contours of the coin impress him: 'yes, tis three pence, I smell the rose' (III.ii.120–1). Such attention to the particulars of coins is absent from the majority of 'city comedies' whose concern is predominantly the way in which all relations are subjected to the law of commodity exchange. In these plays – such as Middleton's *A Mad World my Masters* (published in 1608) – coin, rather than coins, exists as a token of exchange. Correspondingly, the language of other city comedies lacks the textural variation to be found in *The Alchemist*, for words too are used more as equivalents, coins for exchange rather than collection. Thomas Hobbes was to express a view of words as tokens of exchange, of no intrinsic value: 'words are wise mens counters, they do but reckon by them: but they are the mony of fooles'.[1]

Pecuniary metaphors for language are so common as to be dead. We speak of word 'coining' and linguistic 'currency'. Word coining, and the exhilaration of it, are much in evidence in *The Alchemist.* Dapper is as eager to acquire and display a new word as the watch of which he claims to have been robbed. 'What do you think of me', he asks Face who has urged discretion, 'That I am a *Chiause*?' 'What's that?' asks Face, with the rest of us. 'The Turk was, here – /As one would say, do you think I am a Turk?' (I.ii.25–7). Kastril, called upon to quarrel with Surly, is moderately inventive. He calls Kastril 'a shad, a whit,/A very tim' (IV.vii.45–6). Were this one-sided *flyting* match to develop we would expect more dictionary-eluding words.

The world of this play is cognate with that of the 'coney-catching' pamphlets of Dekker and Greene which provided the respectable (and expanding) reading public with titillating access to thieves'

[1] Thomas Hobbes, *Leviathan* (1651), ed. C. B. Macpherson, Harmondsworth, 1968, p. 106.

(coney-catchers') practices, including their 'cant' or jargon.[1] Surly, himself a card-sharp, knows this world and its language well enough; he sustains the coney-catching metaphor throughout his commentary in II.iii. As far as he is concerned the alchemical jargon used by Subtle and Face is another exclusive language of the same sort: 'What a brave language here is? Next to canting?' (II.iii.42).

Word-lover Dapper 'Consorts with the small poets of the time' and can 'court/His mistress out of Ovid' (I.ii.52, 57–58). Sir Epicure Mammon's love of eloquence is on a grander scale. He imagines himself able to purchase the word-power of others:

> my flatterers
> Shall be the pure, and gravest of Divines,
> That I can get for money. My mere fools,
> Eloquent burgesses, and then my poets,
> The same that writ so subtly of the fart,
> Whom I will entertain, still, for that subject.'
> (II.ii.59–64)

For Mammon the worth of words lies in the glamour of their surface effects, not in their meaning. Webster's Duchess of Malfi does not lose sight of the fact of death when she contemplates its various forms:

> What would it pleasure me to have my throat cut
> With diamonds? or to be smothered
> With cassia? or to be shot to death with pearls?
> (IV.ii.216–18)

But one can imagine Mammon relishing the prospect of deaths so expensive, as if the instruments could confer luxury. His use of words is sensual and associative – poetic, in fact – not a matter of settled equivalences. 'I'll geld you, Lungs' he promises Face as a coda to his offer to make him keeper of his seraglio (II.ii.34). It is as if gelding, just a semitone down from gilding, were a form of decoration. And he relishes the prospect of walking naked between 'succubae' (II.ii.48) with no thought of the spiritual peril involved in copulating with she-devils. He produces the word as if it had no meaning other than its sound with its promise of fellatio and other sexual suckings.

We, of course, should be able to hear and understand what Mammon does not: the violence, the extravagance of his language are indices of his contrariness to nature. His desire to eat 'the swelling unctuous paps/Of a fat pregnant sow, newly cut off' (II.ii.83–4) – his own sensual paraphrase of a real Roman recipe

[1] For a description of this *genre* see Brian Gibbons, *Jacobean City Comedy*, London, 1968, Appendix.

– shows his opposition to life and fecundity at the same time as it expresses his rapacious, acquisitive enjoyment of them. Implicit in Jonson's characterisation through language is a moral commentary. But for all the affinities between this – and other 'city comedies' – and medieval morality drama,[1] the energy of this play's language is not primarily moralistic. Mammon, in his relish for language, is allied to the amorally magnanimous Lovewit who, though dramatically a *deus ex machina*, is revealed by his name to be the presiding genius of the play.

Mammon's love of wit expresses itself in overt applause. He exalts the menial 'Lungs' to the status of a classical nature deity – 'Zephyrus' – then asks if the 'bolt's head' 'Blushes'. Quick off the cue Face replies, 'Like a wench with child, sir,/That were, but now, discovered to her master'. 'Excellent witty Lungs!' comes Mammon's gratified response (II.ii.9–11). Face also engages Subtle in a metaphor match, capping Subtle in imagery as in all else:

SUBTLE He looks in that deep ruff, like a head in a platter,
Served in by a short cloak upon two trestles!
FACE Or, what do you say to a collar of brawn, cut down
Beneath the souse, and wriggled with a knife?
(IV.iii.24–7)[2]

One of the few anecdotes to link Jonson with Shakespeare relates that Shakespeare gave a spoon made of the alloy, latten, to one of Jonson's children as a christening gift. He then played on the consonance 'latten'/'Latin' and on Jonson's reputation as a classical scholar: 'Now you expect a great matter. But I shall give you a latten spoon, and you shall translate it' – presumably into some purer, more costly metal.[3] In *The Alchemist*, though the lead and iron brought to Face and Subtle remain steadfastly themselves, a transmutation of language is constantly at work. The word play – some of it silent as the cue for Dol on 'common' – by which one meaning is intended and another heard, subjects the language to the same kind of transformative poundings that the alchemist applies to his metals. L. A. Beaurline has written of Jonson's ability 'to vary, to press a matter to its greatest potential'.[4] He is describing Jonson's plotting but this economy – this pressing of finite materials into new combinations – is equally at work in Jonson's use of language. Surly, in his cod Spanish, speaks of '*la señora . . . como la*

[1] See Gibbons (op. cit.) for this subject; also Alan C. Dessen, '*The Alchemist*: Jonson's "Estates" Play', *Renaissance Drama*, vii (1964), pp. 35–54.
[2] Cf. the metaphor match between Hal and Falstaff in *Henry IV part i*, I.ii.71–9.
[3] *H.&S.*, vol. i, pp. 184–5; the quotation is from *Archdeacon Plume's Notes on Jonson*.
[4] L. A. Beaurline, *Jonson and Elizabethan Comedy*, San Marino, 1978, p. 203.

bien aventuranza de mi vida.' Face picks up, '*Mi vida?* 'Slid, Subtle, he puts me in mind o' the widow' (IV.iii.61–3). Here dialogue, and also plot, are driven forward by an associative momentum. In an earlier scene Mammon and Face discuss the availability of 'stuff' on which to project:

FACE Buy
The covering off o' churches.
. . .
Let 'em stand bare, as do their auditory.

From the idea of the hatless congregation comes the metaphor of churches with hats on:

Or cap 'em, new, with shingles. (II.ii.13–16)

Subtle, basing his explanation of the alchemical process on the writings of Martin Delrio, describes the totality of substances as existing in an extended continuum:

for 'twere absurd
To think that nature, in the earth, bred gold
Perfect, i' the instant. Something went before.
There must be remote matter. (II.iii.137–40)

This concept of a continuum in which some matter is 'remote', some near, is also implicit in several contemporary descriptions of verbal wit. See, for example, George Puttenham's account of the rhetorical figure *metalepsis*:

> which I call the *farfet*, as when we had rather fetch a word a great way off then to vse one nerer hand to expresse the matter aswel & plainer . . . leaping ouer the heads of a great many words, we take one that is furdest off, to vtter our matter by.[1]

Such 'leaping' is *not* what Subtle and Delrio have in mind. The alchemist's journey is more dogged:

Nor can this remote matter, suddenly,
Progress so from extreme, unto extreme,
As to grow gold, and leap o'er all the means.
Nature doth, first, beget th' imperfect; then
Proceeds she to the perfect. (II.iii.155–9)

But Mammon, who will buy rather than make the stone (II.ii.98–101) thinks of money as a way of abbreviating the alchemist's systematic route. Money acts like verbal wit, 'leaping over' intermediaries to fetch in what was remote. Samuel Johnson famously, and derogatively, defined wit as

[1] George Puttenham, *The Arte of English Poesie*, ed. Gladys Doidge Willcock and Alice Walker, Cambridge, 1936, p. 183.

> a kind of *discordia concors*; a combination of dissimilar images, or discovery of occult resemblances in things apparently unlike . . . [in which] the most heterogeneous ideas are yoked by violence together . . .[1]

Mammon's rapacious purchase is an attempt at this kind of violence.

Nevertheless, the Italian poetic theorist, Emmanuele Tesauro, found a divine precedent for poetic wit in a God who 'dwells in the marshes and in the stars, and from the most sordid made the most divine of corporeal creatures'.[2] The wit of this lies in the abridgement of the gap between marshes and stars. Such a model might dignify the kind of social transformations which Subtle performs, 'translating' Face from the 'scarab' who picked over dunghills in search of clothes (I.i.34) to the more exalted 'suburb captain'. It is the parallel of the process which makes gold of metallic faeces (II.iii.62). This wit which exalts the base (and may equally debase the exalted) operates on every level of the play. Mammon's dialogue with Surly moves from the unironic mention of 'stout Marses . . . [and] . . . young Cupids' to the prostitutes of Pict-Hatch whose 'fire' is not only passion, but also inflammation and infection. But Surly sticks to Mammon's language, making the prostitutes the 'decayed Vestals . . . That keep the fire alive' (II.i.61–3). It is only by means of this metaphorical bridge that Mammon is then prompted to speak of infections.

Two divergent pressures – one towards diversity and fragmentation, the other towards unity, uniformity and identity – are operating on various levels in *The Alchemist.* Alchemy is itself predicated on the idea of the fundamental unity – not just continuity – of the material world. By transforming baser metals into the gold to which they aspire it is as if their 'true natures' were recovered. The neurologist Oliver Sacks, in describing the response to the anti-Parkinsonian drug L-Dopa, writes about the 'debased metaphysics' which looks for a miracle drug to 'restore' a lost state of perfect health and happiness – a golden age. 'Mysticism', he enlarges in a note, 'arises by taking analogy for identity – turning similes and metaphors (or 'as' statements) into absolutes (or 'is' statements), converting a useful epistemology into 'absolute truth'.[3] One can see such thinking, with its collapse of distinctions, in practice as Sir Epicure Mammon appropriates every myth available to him and reduces each to a description of alchemy:

[1] from the life of Cowley in Samuel Johnson, *Lives of the English Poets*, ed. G. B. Hill, Oxford, 1905, vol. i, p. 20.

[2] Emmanuele Tesauro, *Il Cannocchiale Aristotelico*, Turin, 1670, p. 584; this passage is translated by S. L. Bethell in 'Gracian, Tesauro and the nature of Metaphysical Wit', in *Northern Miscellany*, i, 1953, p. 33.

[3] Oliver W. Sacks, *Awakenings*, Harmondsworth, 1976, p. 50.

> I'll show you a book, where Moses, and his sister,
> And Solomon have written, of the art;
> Ay, and a treatise penned by Adam . . .
> . . .
> . . . I have a piece of Jason's fleece, too,
> Which was no other, than a book of alchemy,
> . . .
> . . . this, th' Hesperian garden, Cadmus' story,
> Jove's shower, the boon of Midas, Argus' eyes,
> Boccace his Demogorgon, thousands more,
> All abstract riddles of our stone . . .
> (II.i.81–3; 89–90; 101–4)

Sacks expands on the kind of mysticism – a 'mystical holism' – of which alchemy is an example:

> [it] asserts that the world is an entirely uniform and undifferentiated mass of 'world-stuff', 'primal matter', or plasm . . . The therapeutic correlate of such a monist mysticism is the notion of an all-purpose drug, a Panacea or Catholicon, a Quintessential extract of World-Stuff or Brain-Stuff, absolutely pure bottled Goodness or Godness (or Guinness) – de Quincey's 'portable ecstasy corked up in a pink-bottle'.[1]

Or the Philosopher's Stone?

The ur-matter on which the theory of alchemy is predicated is matched by the myth of an original language: the language used by Adam when he gave each creature its name; a language without universals in which every name is a proper name. For all the irrepressible verbal and idiomatic diversity in *The Alchemist* the play and its personnel do suggest the possibility of such an original language – whether the High German that some contemporary philologists had claimed for Adam (II.i.84) or the more traditional Hebrew (II.v.17). Subtle hints at the Adamic state in which every name is a proper name and every proper name is unique (a recipe for incomprehensibility) when he seems to identify Ananias with 'the varlet/That cozened the Apostles' (II.v.72–3). The same may be said of Kastril's delighted response to Subtle's 'Pray God, your sister prove but pliant'. 'Why,/Her name is so' (IV.iv.89–90).

But the best-preserved and most communicative ancient language is the body language in which Dol is particularly fluent. She is urged to 'tickle [the Spaniard] with [her] mother-tongue' since 'His great/Verdugoship has not a jot of language' (III.iii.70–1). The couplings of sexual union are presented as a form of wit. Mammon,

[1] ibid., pp. 50–1.

hot for Dol, asks if there is 'No means,/No trick, to give a man a taste of her – wit – /Or so?' (II.iii.258–60). And Lovewit, asking us to consider 'What a young wife, and a good brain may do' (V.v.155), suggests a kind of equation between sexual resourcefulness and more cerebral wit. The wit of sex – like the wit of money – lies in its power to abridge distances and unite the diverse.

Dol is the 'common wealth' of Face and Subtle; she is also their 'republic' (*res publica*: common thing) (I.i.110). The conflicting pressures – the one towards unity, concord and monoglossia, the other towards diversity, faction and jargon – have their political counterparts in the commonwealth to which the trio (and Mammon) aspire and the civil war to which their competitive individualism gives rise. The 'venture tripartite' between Dol, Face and Subtle declared 'All things in common./Without priority' (I.i.135–6). This egality is under strain at the outset of the play; by the end of Act II faction is entrenched.[1]

While ideas of commonwealth and civil war emerge in the play they are not its central concern. However, with hindsight it is possible to see the play casting a forward shadow across events in England thirty years later. It enables one to understand how Thomas Hobbes' fear of metaphor – his insistence upon settled significations – was of a piece with his horror of civil war:

> The Light of humane minds is Perspicuous Words, but by exact definitions first snuffed, and purged from ambiguity . . . Metaphors, and senslesse and ambiguous words are like *ignes fatui*; and reasoning upon them, is wandering amongst innumerable absurdities; and their end, contention, and sedition, or contempt.[2]

But Hobbes can't keep metaphor out; the irony of 'snuffed' and '*ignes fatui*' may be mournful but it is not accidental. And in much of his work Hobbes' acquaintance Ben Jonson appears to celebrate (or at least indulge in) what he censures. But *The Alchemist*, with Lovewit as the presiding genius, is less censorious than most, and the wit which half-heartedly repairs the divisions of language ('half-heartedly' because those divisions are what feed it) can make something even of stains – such as the 'poesies of the candle' which Lovewit finds on his ceiling (V.v.41).

[1] See Note on Anabaptists, p. xxviii.
[2] *Leviathan*, ed. cit., pp. 116–17.

PLOTTING AND STAGECRAFT

When we mean to build,
We first survey the plot, then draw the model,
And when we see the figure of the house,
Then must we rate the cost of the erection,
Which if we find outweighs ability,
What do we then but draw anew the model
In fewer offices, or at least desist
To build at all? Much more, in this great work –
Which is almost to pluck a kingdom down
And set another up – should we survey
The plot of situation and the model,
Consent upon a sure foundation,
Question surveyors, know our own estate,
How able such a work to undergo,
To weigh against his opposite.

(*Henry IV:2*, I.iii.41–55)

Two kinds of plot are referred to in this speech by Shakespeare's Lord Bardolph; a third covertly. Ben Jonson had practical experience of all three. As a known Catholic, but also a known patriot, he earned the commission to seek out a Catholic priest with knowledge of the Gunpowder Plot. He was to give this priest safe conduct to the Lords where he would be expected to report on the conspiracy. Jonson was unable to find a priest ready to admit to such dangerous knowledge, but he did discover the flaw in the plot. There were too many involved. He reported that as many as 500 were 'enweaved' in the plot.[1] Leaks were inevitable.

Jonson also knew about that more ordinary kind of plotting with which Lord Bardolph illustrates his conspiracy theory. Whether or not Jonson underwent an apprenticeship to his step-father's trade of bricklaying, he was clearly able to follow the 'plots' or groundplans of houses – such as the one of his shop that Abel Drugger hands to Subtle in order to discover 'Which way [he] should make [his] door . . . And, where [his] shelves' (I.iii.11–12). Jonson applies a builder's constructive skills to his writing. See, for example, his dry-stone-wall theory of syntax:

> The congruent, and harmonious fitting of parts in a sentence, hath almost the fastning, and force of knitting, and connexion: As in stones well squar'd, which will rise strong a great way without mortar.[2]

And Jonson knew about plotting plays (Shakespeare's covert metaphor in Lord Bardolph's speech). Coleridge thought *The*

[1] *H.&S.*, vol. i, p. 41.
[2] *H.&S.*, vol. viii, p. 623.

Alchemist, along with the *Oedipus Tyrannus* and *Tom Jones*, to be the three 'most perfect plots ever planned'.[1] *The Alchemist*'s plot is to some extent devised by its central characters – Dol, Subtle and Face – who are involved in a series of intersecting plots to defraud their willing gulls. But though the play comprises a series of mini-plots (conspiracies), the plot (temporal design) of the play is not coterminous with these. For Kenneth Tynan *The Alchemist* is 'a good episodic play . . . Like bead after bead the episodes click together upon the connecting string, which is chicanery and chiselry.'[2] But while the protagonists' plots are multiple, Jonson's plot is single. W. B. Yeats wrote that 'a poem comes right with a click like a closing box.'[3] And for all the lesser clicks which Tynan describes it is with such a single click that this play's plot closes: the click of a trap springing shut as the coney-catchers are caught. 'I am catched', says Face for whom there is nothing left but confession and the hope of a new bargain (V.iii.75). This is the moment at which Jonson's single plot overtakes the several plots of the trio. Face's face-saving lie to the colleagues he betrays – 'I sent for him, indeed' (V.iv.129) – attempts to gloss over the fact that there was a move unforeseen by this master plotter.

An image of the play's momentum can be found in the progress of the supposed – though offstage – alchemical projection which Subtle feigns to be performing at Mammon's behest. It is a process of progressive elaboration and complication, culminating, not in the desired Philosopher's Stone, but in a noisy explosion (IV.v.55). Face's reaction at this point unknowingly foreshadows his genuine discomforture later when the unforeseen explodes:

> O sir, we are defeated! All the works
> Are flown *in fumo*: every glass is burst.
> Furnace, and all rent down!
>
> (IV.v.57–9)

Two scenes later he is to say in earnest 'We are undone, and taken' (IV.vii.114).

At the start of the play the various gulls (each of whom demands a different style of approach) file in, one or two at a time, allowing Face to change face and habit, Subtle to modify his tone, and Dol to switch as need calls from Fairy Queen to distracted gentlewoman. But this initially orderly and manageable sequence speeds up. The order quickens and becomes unpredictable, demanding more and

[1] *Coleridge's Table Talk and Omniana*, Oxford, 1917, p. 312.

[2] Kenneth Tynan, 'A Slamming of Doors' (1950) in R. V. Holdsworth, *Jonson: Every Man in his Humour and The Alchemist: A Casebook*, London, 1978, p. 224.

[3] *Letters on Poetry from W. B. Yeats to Dorothy Wellesley*, Oxford, 1964, p. 22.

more resourceful improvisation of the trio. At the play's half-way point (III.iii.) Face has returned from the Temple where Surly has failed to turn up, having instead arrived at the house disguised as the Spaniard whom Subtle now proposes to con with Dol's help. But just as Dol is about to 'tune her virginal' in readiness, Dapper turns up – late. Dol now has to dress as the Queen of Fairy and Subtle to get out of his alchemist's habit to become her priest. But no sooner is this underway than Drugger and Kastril arrive, eager to see, not the Priest of Fairy, but the 'Doctor'. Face now manages momentarily to clear the scene for Dapper's encounter with his 'aunt' by dispatching Kastril and Drugger in search of widow Pliant. But the fairy buzzing has barely started before Mammon's unexpected arrival demands a halt. Dapper is neutralised in desperate fashion – he is shoved in the privy with a gingerbread gag in his mouth.

Act IV begins with Mammon being hurried off with Dol who has stopped buzzing (and changed clothes) in order to spout Broughton while Face is left to cope with Kastril and his sister. But he has no time to change from alchemist's bellows-man (Mammon's friend 'Lungs') into the Captain Face that Kastril knows. Now he prays 'for a suit,/To fall . . ., like a curtain: flap' (IV.ii.6–7). But this is beyond even Face who is now put to the expert actor's test of having nothing – no prop – but himself with which to create the required illusion.

In the play's early scenes we take pleasure in the conspirators' control – in their ability to orchestrate events. As matters become more complicated and their gulls arrive late, early, not at all or unexpectedly, the pleasure we take is in watching their ability to improvise – as when Face brilliantly directs Kastril in his first practical quarrelling lesson, and then when Ananias turns up gives him too grounds to join in with theological denunciation, thus averting – by drowning out – the exposure which Surly is about to perform.

Jonson's language is so exciting and so various that a *reader* of this play might neglect its sheer *theatrical* brilliance. The pace and pitch of this play cannot be ignored in performance. Jonson's timing is impeccable – as when Ananias enters at the height of the uproar of the engineered quarrel with the words 'Peace to the household' (IV.vii.42). No auditor can ignore the noise that this play makes: the series of knocks, the explosion, the cry of the forgotten Dapper when his gingerbread gag has gone.

There are only two stage directions in the Quarto edition of *The Alchemist: Within* at II.i.25 and *Dol is seen* at II.iii.210 – the moment after Mammon has provided an inadvertent cue on 'common'. Such is the thrift of Jonson's writing that other stage directions are implicit and would be *discovered* by any full-witted actor in the course of performance. (For example 'Who's there?' [I.ii.162] clearly implies the direction – *One knocks without* – that Jonson added in Folio.) The several stage directions added to the Folio edition of the play clarify the situation for the reader but are, strictly speaking, superfluous. The economy of good stage writing demands that the actions be implicit in the words.

Thrift – making a little go a long way (no need to call Dol when 'common' has already been sounded) – is essential to good plotting; the Gunpowder Plot might have succeeded with fewer participants. Thrift is also necessary to the practical art of theatre. The Spanish costume which Drugger borrows from some actors pays its way like any worthy item in a theatre wardrobe – by adapting to a number of occasions. Whoever marries the widow must first 'become' the Spanish grandee by climbing into this costume. Like so much else in the play – Mammon's metalware, Dame Pliant herself – the range of this costume's potential is possessed and tried in fantasy before being finally realized by Lovewit.

This grandee's costume had an earlier life as a 'Hieronimo's cloak and hat'. Here is another link between Lovewit and his Blackfriars-dwelling creator, for Jonson is reputed to have played the part of Hieronimo in Kyd's *The Spanish Tragedy* (for which he also wrote additions). For all his professed loathing of the stuff and trumpery of theatrical shows, Jonson knew how to put them to use.

NOTE ON ANABAPTISTS

The Anabaptists whom Jonson satirizes with no trace of affection were, historically, egalitarians. During the occupation of Münster John of Leyden declared that 'all things were to be in common, there was to be no private property and nobody was to do any more work, but simply trust in God' (Norman Cohen, *The Pursuit of the Millenium*, London, 1957, p. 288). Leyden's ideal (which he contradicted by becoming a crowned tyrant) is very close to that expressed by the good Gonzalo in Shakespeare's *The Tempest*:

> I' th' commonwealth I would by contraries
> Execute all things; for no kind of traffic
> Would I admit; no name of magistrate;
> . . . .
> All things in common Nature should produce
> Without sweat or endeavour . . . (II.i.143–5; 155–6)

For all Gonzalo's benignity, his companions are right to point out the flaw in his thinking – 'No sovereignty', he says, 'And yet he would be King'.

The Tempest was probably written shortly after *The Alchemist* and, with its magus protagonist, it looks at utopianism less cynically than does the earlier play to which Gonzalo's 'all things in common' may be a reference. But it is possibly informed, as *The Alchemist* certainly is, by the Anabaptist experiment in communal living.

NOTE ON THE TEXT

The Alchemist was first printed in quarto (Q) in 1612 and then included in the folio (F) edition of Jonson's *Works* in 1616. Jonson supervised the publication of both editions and it is likely that the copy text used for F was a corrected edition of Q. A second folio edition of the *Works* (F2) came out in 1640 and included some emendations. The present edition is based on F in all but a few details and all substantive variations from Q are recorded in the textual notes. Many of these variations stem from the tightening of regulations in the intervening years over the uttering of religious material on stage. Hence oaths which might be found blasphemous were emended in F to pagan or secular equivalents. For instance, 'God's will' (Q) becomes 'Death on me' in F (I.i.149). I have retained all these emendations (though there is a case for scrapping them) except one, at I.ii.56, which makes no sense outside the context of censorship.

Jonson's comprehensible punctuation in F has largely been retained, but spelling – except when the word was archaic or odd at the time – has been modernized. Jonson's liberal use of capitals and italics has been abandoned here – with some regret since the typography of F gives an edge to many words which, while not necessarily specialist, smack of jargon or restricted use. I have, however, retained Jonson's use of black-letter type for German words – too good a visual joke to miss. All editorial stage directions are in square brackets; any others are as in F. In F block entries of all participants precede each scene with the name of the first speaker at the beginning. Here entries are supplied as the action requires and all speech prefixes are ranged on the left. (Jonson distributes the prefixes within the line where a metrical line is shared by more than one character.)

FURTHER READING

Barton, Anne, *Ben Jonson, Dramatist*, Cambridge, 1984.
Barish, Jonas, *Ben Jonson and the Language of Prose Comedy*, Cambridge, Mass., 1960.
Beaurline, L. A., *Jonson and Elizabethan Comedy*, San Marino, 1978.
Blissett, W. and Van Fossen, R. W. edd., *A Celebration of Ben Jonson*, London 1973.
Craig, D. H., ed., *Ben Jonson: the Critical Heritage 1599–1798*, London, 1990.
Dessen, Alan C., '*The Alchemist:* Jonson's "Estates" Play', *Renaissance Drama*, vii, 1964, pp. 35–54.
Duncan, Edgar Hill, 'Jonson's *Alchemist* and the Literature of Alchemy', *PMLA*, lxi, 1946, pp. 699–710.
Eliot, T. S., 'Ben Jonson', in *The Sacred Wood*, London, 1920.
Gibbons, Brian, *Jacobean City Comedy*, 1968, rev. ed., London, 1980.
Holdsworth, R. V., ed., *Jonson: Every Man in his Humour and The Alchemist: a Casebook*, London, 1978.
Hoy, Cyrus, 'The Pretended Piety of Jonson's *Alchemist*', *Renaissance Papers*, 1957, pp. 15–19.
Hyland, Peter, *Disguise and Role-Playing in Ben Jonson's Drama*, Salzburg, 1977.
Kay, W. David, *Ben Jonson: a Literary Life*, Basingstoke, 1995.
Kernan, Alvin, 'Alchemy and Acting: the Major Plays of Ben Jonson', in *Ben Jonson: Quadricentennial Essays*, ed. Mary Olive Thomas, Atlanta, 1973.
Knights, L. C., *Drama and Society in the Age of Jonson*, London, 1937.
Levin, Harry, 'Two Magian Comedies: *The Tempest* and *The Alchemist*', *Shakespeare Survey*, xxii, 1969, pp. 47–58.
Mebane, John S., *Renaissance Magic and the Return of the Golden Age*, Lincoln (Nebraska) and London, 1989. Chapter 7, 'The Renaissance Magus as Mock-Hero: Utopianism and Religious Enthusiasm in Ben Jonson's *The Alchemist*' was earlier published as an article in *Renaissance Drama*, x, 1979, pp 117–139.
Miles, Rosalind, *Ben Jonson: his Crafts and Art*, London, 1990.
Partridge, E. B., *The Broken Compass*, London 1958.
Riggs, David, *Ben Jonson: A Life*, Cambridge, Mass., 1989.
Roberts, Gareth, *The Mirror of Alchemy: Alchemical Ideas and Images in Manuscripts and Books*, London, 1994.

THE
ALCHEMIST.

A Comœdie.

Acted in the yeere 1610. By the
Kings MAIESTIES
Seruants.

The Author B. I.

LVCRET.

——*petere inde coronam,*
Vnde priùs nulli velarint tempora Musæ.

LONDON,
Printed by WILLIAM STANSBY

M. DC. XVI.

Sweeney, John G., *Jonson and the Psychology of Public Theater*, Princetown, 1985.
Watson, Robert N., Ben Jonson's Parodic Strategy, Cambridge, Mass., 1987.
Womack, Peter, *Ben Jonson*, Oxford, 1986.

TO THE LADY, MOST DESERVING HER NAME, AND BLOOD: Mary, LADY WROTH

MADAM,

In the age of sacrifices, the truth of religion was not in the greatness, and fat of the offerings, but in the devotion, and zeal of the sacrificers: else, what could a handful of gums have done in the sight of a hecatomb? Or, how might I appear at this altar, except with those affections, that no less love the light and witness, than they have the conscience of your virtue? If what I offer bear an acceptable odour, and hold the first strength, it is your value of it, which remembers, where, when, and to whom it was kindled. Otherwise, as the times are, there comes rarely forth that thing, so full of authority, or example, but by assiduity and custom, grows less, and loses. This, yet, safe in your judgment (which is a Sidney's) is forbidden to speak more; lest it talk, or look like one of the ambitious faces of the time: who, the more they paint, are the less themselves.

Your Ladyship's true honourer,
Ben Jonson.

2–3 *DESERVING . . . BLOOD* most aequall with vertue, and her Blood: The Grace, and Glory of women Q

10–12 *Or, how . . . virtue?* Or how, yet, might a grateful minde be furnish'd against the iniquitie of Fortune; except, when she fail'd it, it had power to impart it selfe? A way found out, to ouercome euen those, whom Fortune hath enabled to returne most, since they, yet leaue themselues more. In this assurance am I planted; and stand with those affections at this Altar, as shall no more auoide the light and witnesse, then they do the conscience of your vertue Q

14 *value of it, which* valew, that Q

15 *as the times are* in these times Q

17 *assiduity* daylinesse Q

18 *This, yet* But this Q

4–5 *Mary, LADY WROTH* daughter of Robert Sidney, first Earl of Leicester, and niece of Sir Philip Sidney; she married Sir Robert Wroth in 1604. The name was also spelled 'Worth' — hence 'deserving her name'

7–12 from Seneca, *De Beneficiis*, i.vi.2

9 *gums* incense

10 *hecatomb* huge public sacrifice

12 *conscience* consciousness

20 *paint* use make up

TO THE READER

If thou beest more, thou art an understander, and then I trust thee. If thou art one that takest up, and but a pretender, beware at what hands thou receivest thy commodity; for thou wert never more fair in the way to be cozened (than in this age) in poetry, especially in plays: wherein, now, the concupiscence of jigs and dances so reigneth, as to run away from nature, and be afraid of her, is the only point of art that tickles the spectators. But how out of purpose, and place, do I name art? When the professors are grown so obstinate contemners of it, and presumers on their own naturals, as they are deriders of all diligence that way, and, by simple mocking at the terms, when they understand not the things, think to get off wittily with their ignorance. Nay, they are esteemed the more learned, and sufficient for this, by the multitude, through their excellent vice of judgment. For they commend writers, as they do fencers, or wrestlers; who if they come in robustiously, and put for it with a great deal of violence, are received for the braver fellows: when many times their own rudeness is the cause of their disgrace, and a little touch of their adversary gives all that boisterous force the foil. I deny not, but that these men, who always seek to do more than enough, may some time happen on something that is good, and great; but very seldom: and when it comes it doth not recompense the rest of their ill. It sticks out perhaps, and is more eminent, because all is sordid, and vile about it: as lights are more discerned in a thick darkness, than a faint shadow. I speak not this, out of a hope to do good on any man, against his will; for I know, if it were put to the question of theirs, and mine, the worse would find more suffrages: because the most favour common errors. But I give thee this warning, that there is a great difference between those, that (to gain the opinion of copie) utter all they can, however unfitly; and those that use election, and a mean. For it is only the disease of the unskilful, to think rude things greater than polished: or scattered more numerous than composed.

This preface is taken from the British Library Q. It was not included in F A more expanded version of these views (which derive from Quintilian) can be found in Jonson's *Discoveries* (*H. & S.* viii, esp. pp. 583, 586–7)

---

1 *To the Reader . . . than composed* Q; not in F
more i.e. more than a reader
10 *naturals* what nature has given them (with a pun on 'fools')
17 *braver* finer
30 *copie* copiousness *all they can* all they know (ken)
31 *those that use election, and a mean* those that employ discrimination and moderation

THE PERSONS OF THE PLAY

SUBTLE, The Alchemist
FACE, The Housekeeper
DOL COMMON, Their Colleague
DAPPER, A Clerk
DRUGGER, A Tobaccoman
LOVEWIT, Master of the House

EPICURE MAMMON, A Knight
SURLY, A Gamester
TRIBULATION, A Pastor of Amsterdam
ANANIAS, A Deacon there
KASTRIL, The Angry Boy
DAME PLIANT, His Sister: A Widow

Neighbours
Officers
Mutes

The Scene

LONDON [, inside Lovewit's house and in the street outside]

1 *Play* Comoedie Q
14 The Scene *LONDON* F; not in Q

Tobaccoman tobacco was a new and fashionable commodity and tobacco sellers a new breed of tradesmen. See John Earle, *Microcosmography* (1628) for the 'character' of *A Tobacco Seller*
Kastril an obsolete spelling of 'kestril'. As an 'angry boy' he is one of a type of pugnacious men about town
Mutes non-speaking parts. e.g. the Parson of V.v.118

THE ALCHEMIST

THE ARGUMENT

T he sickness hot, a master quit, for fear,
H is house in town: and left one servant there.
E ase him corrupted, and gave means to know
A cheater, and his punk; who, now brought low,
L eaving their narrow practice, were become
C ozeners at large: and, only wanting some
H ouse to set up, with him they here contract,
E ach for a share, and all begin to act. –
M uch company they draw, and much abuse,
I n casting figures, telling fortunes, news,
S elling of flies, flat bawdry, with the stone:
T ill it, and they, and all in fume are gone.

1 *sickness* plague
4 *punk* whore
10 *casting figures* drawing up horoscopes
11 *stone* the Philosopher's Stone
12 *fume* smoke

PROLOGUE

Fortune, that favours fools, these two short hours
  We wish away; both for your sakes, and ours,
Judging spectators: and desire in place,
  To th'author justice, to ourselves but grace.
Our scene is London, 'cause we would make known,
  No country's mirth is better than our own,
No clime breeds better matter, for your whore,
  Bawd, squire, imposter, many persons more,
Whose manners, now called humours, feed the stage:
  And which have still been subject, for the rage
Or spleen of comic writers. Though this pen
  Did never aim to grieve, but better men;
Howe'er the age, he lives in, doth endure
  The vices that she breeds, above their cure.
But, when the wholesome remedies are sweet,
  And, in their working, gain, and profit meet,
He hopes to find no spirit so much diseased,
  But will, with such fair correctives be pleased.
For here, he doth not fear, who can apply.
  If there be any, that will sit so nigh
Unto the stream, to look what it doth run,
  They shall find things, they'd think, or wish, were done;
They are so natural follies, but so shown.
  As even the doers may see, and yet not own.

10 *for* to Q

---

7 *for* William Empson observes that this must mean 'as providing' and not 'because' ('The Alchemist and the Critics', 1970, in *Casebook* ed. R. V. Holdsworth)

8 *squire* pimp

9 *now called humours* according to medieval psychologists an individual's temperament was determined by the balance and proportion of four bodily humours: blood, phlegm, red bile and black bile. These in turn reflect the balance of the four elements: air, water, fire and earth. A 'humour' thence came to mean any bent of personality. Jonson protests against the misuse of this term (as an excuse for fashionably interesting foibles) in his induction to *Every Man Out of his Humour*, 110–17

12 *better* a verb

19 *apply* interpret veiled allusions

Act I, Scene i

[*Inside Lovewit's house*]

[*Enter*] FACE, SUBTLE, DOL COMMON

FACE
Believ't, I will.
SUBTLE Thy worst. I fart at thee.
DOL
Ha' you your wits? Why gentlemen! For love–
FACE
Sirrah, I'll strip you—
SUBTLE What to do? Lick figs
Out at my—
FACE Rogue, rogue, out of all your sleights.
DOL
Nay, look ye! Sovereign, General, are you madmen?
SUBTLE
O, let the wild sheep loose.
[*threatens* FACE *with phial*]
I'll gum your silks
With good strong water, an' you come.
DOL Will you have
The neighbours hear you? Will you betray all?
Hark, I hear somebody.
FACE Sirrah—
SUBTLE I shall mar
All that the tailor has made, if you approach.
FACE
You most notorious whelp, you insolent slave
Dare you do this?
SUBTLE Yes faith, yes faith.
FACE Why! Who
Am I, my mongrel? Who am I?
SUBTLE I'll tell you,
Since you know not yourself—
FACE Speak lower, rogue.

3 *figs* piles, the *ficus morbus*
6 *gum* stiffen
10 *All that the tailor has made* this establishes that Face's persona has been manufactured

SUBTLE
Yes. You were once (time's not long past) the good,
Honest, plain, livery-three-pound-thrum; that kept
Your master's worship's house, here, in the Friars,
For the vacations—
FACE
Will you be so loud?
SUBTLE
Since, by my means, translated suburb-Captain.
FACE
By your means, Doctor Dog?
SUBTLE
Within man's memory,
All this, I speak of.
FACE
Why, I pray you, have I
Been countenanced by you? Or you, by me?
Do but collect, sir, where I met you first.
SUBTLE
I do not hear well.
FACE
Not of this, I think it.
But I shall put you in mind, sir, at Pie Corner,
Taking your meal of steam in, from cooks' stalls,
Where, like the father of hunger, you did walk
Piteously costive, with your pinched-horn-nose,
And your complexion, of the Roman wash,
Stuck full of black, and melancholic worms,
Like powder corns, shot, at th'artillery-yard.

16 *livery-three-pound-thrum* 'livery' is a servant's garb, 'three-pound' is probably Face's annual wage, and 'thrum' is waste thread – the loose end of a weaver's warp. The whole compound suggests that Face was a lowly menial

17 *the Friars* Blackfriars in London, between St. Paul's and the river; site of the Blackfriars theatre and also of Jonson's home for a time

18 *vacations* between the four terms of the Law-Courts: Hilary (11th–31st January), Easter (mid-April–8th May), Trinity (22nd May–12th June), and Michaelmas (2nd–25th November). There was a lull in London activity during vacations

19 *translated* transformed into

23 *collect* recollect

25 *Pie Corner* a place in nearby Smithfield, noted for cooks' shops

26 *Taking your meal of steam in* Martial I.xcii.7–10

27 *father of hunger* Catullus xxi.1. 'pater esuritionum'

29 *of the Roman wash* a 'wash' is a dye. The Roman wash may be dark like an Italian, or red like the Scarlet Whore of Babylon, as the Roman church was portrayed

31 *powder corns* grains of gunpowder
artillery-yard the exercise yard of the Honourable Artillery Company at Teasel Close (now Artillery Lane). It was also used by the City Trainband (a home guard)

SUBTLE
I wish, you could advance your voice, a little.

FACE
When you went pinned up, in the several rags
You'd raked, and picked from dunghills, before day,
Your feet in mouldy slippers, for your kibes,
A felt of rug, and a thin threaden cloak,
That scarce would cover your no-buttocks—

SUBTLE
So, sir!

FACE
When all your alchemy, and your algebra,
Your minerals, vegetals, and animals,
Your conjuring, cozening, and your dozen of trades,
Could not relieve your corps, with so much linen
Would make you tinder, but to see a fire;
I ga' you countenance, credit for your coals,
Your stills, your glasses, your materials,
Built you a furnace, drew you customers,
Advanced all your black arts; lent you, beside,
A house to practise in—

SUBTLE
Your master's house?

FACE
Where you have studied the more thriving skill
Of bawdry, since.

SUBTLE
Yes, in your master's house.
You, and the rats, here, kept possession.
Make it not strange. I know, y'were one, could keep
The buttr'y-hatch still locked, and save the chippings,
Sell the dole-beer to aqua-vitae-men,
The which, together with your Christmas vails,
At post and pair, your letting out of counters,
Made you a pretty stock, some twenty marks,
And gave you credit, to converse with cobwebs,
Here, since your mistress' death hath broke up house.

35 *kibes* chilblains
36–7 see Martial I.xcii, 7–8
36 *felt of rug* rough wool hat *threaden* made of thread
39 *vegetals* vegetable substances
41 *corps* body
52 *butt'ry-hatch* the buttery was where drink was stored
53 *aqua-vitae-men* liquor dealers
54 *Christmas vails* Christmas boxes, tips
55 *post and pair* a card game
letting out of counters as in roulette now, counters (then usually metal) were used in place of coin for gambling. Face would be tipped for supplying these

FACE
You might talk softlier, rascal.
SUBTLE
No, you scarab,
I'll thunder you, in pieces. I will teach you
How to beware, to tempt a fury again
That carries tempest in his hand, and voice.
FACE
The place has made you valiant.
SUBTLE
No, your clothes.
Thou vermin, have I ta'en thee, out of dung,
So poor, so wretched, when no living thing
Would keep thee company, but a spider, or worse?
Raised thee from brooms, and dust, and wat'ring-pots?
Sublimed thee, and exalted thee, and fixed thee
I' the third region, called our state of grace?
Wrought thee to spirit, to quintessence, with pains
Would twice have won me the philosopher's work?
Put thee in words, and fashion? Made thee fit
For more than ordinary fellowships?
Given thee thy oaths, thy quarrelling dimensions?
Thy rules, to cheat at horse-race, cock-pit, cards,
Dice, or whatever gallant tincture else?
Made thee a second, in mine own great art?
And have I this for thank? Do you rebel?
Do you fly out, i' the projection?
Would you be gone, now?
DOL
Gentlemen, what mean you?
Will you mar all?

69 *our state of grace* the high state of grace Q

---

59 *scarab* dung beetle
68 *Sublimed* converted into vapour to remove impurities
exalted alchemical exaltation is a process of purification and concentration
fixed stabilized
69 *third region* the upper, and purest, region of the air
70 *quintessence* the 'fifth essence' of which heavenly bodies are composed and which is latent in substances composed of the four material elements
71 *philosopher's work* Philosopher's Stone
72–4 *Put thee ... dimensions* taught you how to speak and dress; enabled you to enter company a) better than average b) beyond what you would find at cheap eating houses (ordinaries); taught you how to swear and on what grounds you may quarrel
75 *cock-pit* cock-fighting
76 *gallant tincture* touch of gallantry; *tincture* is an alchemical term
79 *projection* the moment of alchemical transformation when the Philosopher's Stone interpenetrates qualities with the matter to be changed

SUBTLE
Slave, thou hadst had no name—
DOL
Will you undo yourselves, with civil war?
SUBTLE
Never been known, past *equi clibanum*,
The heat of horse-dung, under ground, in cellars,
Or an ale-house, darker than deaf John's: been lost
To all mankind, but laundresses, and tapsters,
Had not I been.
DOL
Do you know who hears you, Sovereign?
FACE
Sirrah—
DOL
Nay, General, I thought you were civil—
FACE
I shall turn desperate, if you grow thus loud.
SUBTLE
And hang thyself, I care not.
FACE
Hang thee, collier,
And all thy pots, and pans, in picture I will,
Since thou hast moved me—
DOL
(O, this'll o'erthrow all.)
FACE
Write thee up bawd, in Paul's; have all thy tricks
Of coz'ning with a hollow coal, dust, scrapings,
Searching for things lost, with a sieve, and shears,
Erecting figures, in your rows of houses,

83 *equi clibanum* lit. 'horse's oven' – horse dung was used by alchemists when a moderate heat was desired

85 *deaf John's* an alehouse (unidentified)

90 *Hang thee, collier* cf. *Twelfth Night* III.iv.119, 'Hang him, foul collier!' (of the devil). It was commonplace to associate colliers with the infernal. Subtle's smoky appearance would suggest the remark

91 *in picture* Face threatens to expose Subtle with a public advertisement

93 *Paul's* St. Paul's Cathedral (not the one now standing); a popular meeting place for secular purposes of social and business exchange. In Dekker's *The Dead Tearme* (1608) Paul's steeple complains 'am I like a common Mart where all Commodities . . . are to be bought and solde' (E^r)

94 *cozening with a hollow coal* Chaucer describes this trick in the *Canon's Yeoman's Tale*, 1159–64. Silver filings are placed inside a hollow coal which is then sealed with wax. When the wax melts molten silver appears amongst the coals to convince prospective clients of the 'alchemist's' prowess

95 *sieve, and shears* the points of shears are stuck into the rim of a sieve to form a dowsing instrument for divination

96 *erecting figures* see *Argument* 10

And taking in of shadows, with a glass,
Told in red letters: and a face, cut for thee,
Worse than Gamaliel Ratsey's.

DOL
Are you sound?
Ha' you your senses, masters?

FACE
I will have
A book, but barely reckoning thy impostures,
Shall prove a true philosopher's stone, to printers.

SUBTLE
Away, you trencher-rascal.

FACE
Out you dog-leech,
The vomit of all prisons—

DOL
Will you be
Your own destructions, gentlemen?

FACE
Still spewed out
For lying too heavy o' the basket.

SUBTLE
Cheater.

FACE
Bawd.

SUBTLE Cow-herd.

FACE
Conjurer.

SUBTLE
Cut-purse.

FACE
Witch.

DOL
O me!
We are ruined! Lost! Ha' you no more regard
To your reputations? Where's your judgment? S'light,
Have yet, some care of me, o' your republic—

FACE
Away this brach. I'll bring thee, rogue, within
The statute of sorcery, *tricesimo tertio*,

97 *glass* a crystal or beryl ball which is supposedly entered by angels which can be discerned and understood by a *speculatrix*

98 *red letters: and a face, cut for thee* eye-catching rubric headings and a wood-cut portrait

99 *Gamaliel Ratsey* a highwayman, hanged in 1605. He worked in a hideous mask, probably referred to here

103 *trencher-rascal* meal-scrounger

104 *dog-leech* dog-doctor (i.e. quack)

106 *For lying too heavy o' the basket* for taking an unfairly large helping from the communal basket of scraps for prisoners

109 *'Slight* 'God's light'

110 *republic* Lat. 'common thing', i.e. Dol

111 *brach* bitch

112–13 *tricesimo tertio . . . Eighth* this act (classified as 33 Henry VIII c.8) was passed in 1541 and forbade, *inter alia*, invocations to find gold or silver and divinations to discover lost or stolen goods. It was repealed in 1863

Of Harry the Eighth: ay, and (perhaps) thy neck
Within a noose, for laund'ring gold, and barbing it.

DOL

You'll bring your head within a coxcomb, will you?

She catcheth out Face his sword: and breaks Subtle's glass

And you, sir, with your menstrue, gather it up.
S'death, you abominable pair of stinkards,
Leave off your barking, and grow one again,
Or, by the light that shines, I'll cut your throats.
I'll not be made a prey unto the marshal,
For ne'er a snarling dog-bolt o' you both.
Ha' you together cozened all this while,
And all the world, and shall it now be said
You've made most courteous shift, to cozen yourselves?
[*To* FACE] You will accuse him? You will bring him in
Within the statute? Who shall take your word?
A whoreson, upstart, apocryphal captain,
Whom not a puritan, in Blackfriars, will trust
So much, as for a feather! [*To* SUBTLE] And you, too,
Will give the cause, forsooth? You will insult,
And claim a primacy, in the divisions?
You must be chief? As if you, only, had
The powder to project with? And the work
Were not begun out of equality?
The venture tripartite? All things in common?
Without priority? 'Sdeath, you perpetual curs,

114 *it* not in Q

---

114 *laundering . . . barbing* washing gold coins in acid to dissolve some of the surface was known as 'laundering'; 'barbing' involved clipping the edges. Tampering with coin was a capital offence

115 *You'll bring your head . . . you?* you're determined to be a fool? The coxcomb (which Dol counterposes to the noose [114]) was the traditional fool's headdress

116 *menstrue* solvent

120 *marshal* provost-marshal, in charge of prisons

121 *dog-bolt* a blunt-headed arrow. Here used figuratively and with an associative logic from 'snarling'

127 *apocryphal* fictional

128–9 *Blackfriars . . . feather!* many Puritans lived in Blackfriars. Surprisingly they were the principal purveyors of feathers and plumes – a fact that let them in for much satire

133 *powder to project with* here used figuratively for criminal inventiveness

136 *'Sdeath* 'God's death'

Fall to your couples again, and cozen kindly,
And heartily, and lovingly, as you should,
And lose not the beginning of a term,
Or, by this hand, I shall grow factious too,
And take my part, and quit you.

FACE
'Tis his fault,
He ever murmurs, and objects his pains,
And says, the weight of all lies upon him.

SUBTLE
Why, so it does.

DOL
How does it? Do not we
Sustain our parts?

SUBTLE
Yes, but they are not equal.

DOL
Why, if your part exceed today, I hope
Ours may, tomorrow, match it.

SUBTLE
Ay, they may.

DOL
May, murmuring mastiff? Ay, and do. Death on me!
Help me to throttle him.

SUBTLE
Dorothy, mistress Dorothy,
'Ods precious, I'll do anything. What do you mean?

DOL
Because o' your fermentation, and cibation?

SUBTLE
Not I, by heaven—

DOL
Your Sol, and Luna—[*To* FACE] help me.

SUBTLE
Would I were hanged then. I'll conform myself.

DOL
Will you, sir, do so then, and quickly: swear.

SUBTLE
What should I swear?

DOL
To leave your faction, sir.

149 *Death on me* Gods will Q

---

137 *couples* the word used for a pair of hunting dogs working together
cozen kindly deceive amicably (with a pun on 'act like relatives')
139 *term* of the law courts. The four terms were periods of great business and social activity and provided opportunities for swindlers
142 *objects* 'puts forward' (a Latinism)
150 *'Ods precious* 'God's precious [blood]'
151 *fermentation . . . cibation* the sixth and seventh processes of alchemy
152 *Sol, and Luna* gold and silver; each metal was associated with a planet
155 *faction* quarrel

And labour, kindly, in the common work.

SUBTLE
Let me not breathe, if I meant ought, beside.
I only used those speeches, as a spur
To him.

DOL I hope we need no spurs, sir. Do we?

FACE
'Slid, prove today, who shall shark best.

SUBTLE Agreed.

DOL
Yes, and work close, and friendly.

SUBTLE 'Slight, the knot
Shall grow the stronger, for this breach, with me.

DOL
Why so, my good baboons! Shall we go make
A sort of sober, scurvy, precise neighbours,
(That scarce have smiled twice, sin' the king came in)
A feast of laughter, at our follies? Rascals,
Would run themselves from breath, to see me ride,
Or you t'have but a hole, to thrust your heads in,
For which you should pay ear-rent? No, agree.
And may Don Provost ride a-feasting, long,
In his old velvet jerkin, and stained scarves
(My noble Sovereign, and worthy General)
Ere we contribute a new crewel garter
To his most worsted worship.

SUBTLE Royal Dol!
Spoken like Claridiana, and thy self!

160 *'Slid* 'God's [eye] lid'
shark swindle

164 *sort of* set of
precise puritanical; strict in religious observance

165 *sin' the king came in* i.e. since 1603

167–9 *to see ... ear-rent* to see me displayed in a cart as a prostitute and you pilloried and your ears cut off. (Dee's assistant Kelley lost both ears as a punishment for coining)

170 *Don Provost* Provost-marshal 'who is often both Informer, Judge, and Executioner ... [and] punishes disorderlie Souldiors, Coyners, Free-booters, highway robbers ...' Cotgrave, *A Dictionary of the French and English Tongues*, London, 1611. Dol here evokes the hangman, entitled to the clothes of his victims

173–4 *crewel garter ... worsted worship* two puns playing on 'crewel' (yarn and 'cruel') and 'worsted' (dressed in worsted and 'thwarted')

175 *Claridiana* heroine of Diego Ortuñez del Calahorra's *Caballero del Sol*, a popular romance first translated as *The Mirror of Princely Deeds and Knighthood*, 1578

FACE
For which, at supper, thou shalt sit in triumph,
And not be styled Dol Common, but Dol Proper,
Dol Singular: the longest cut, at night,
Shall draw thee for his Dol Particular.

[*A bell rings*]

SUBTLE
Who's that? One rings. To the window, Dol. Pray
heaven,
The master do not trouble us, this quarter.

FACE
O, fear not him. While there dies one, a week,
O'the plague, he's safe, from thinking toward London.
Beside, he's busy at his hop-yards, now:
I had a letter from him. If he do,
He'll send such word, for airing o' the house
As you shall have sufficient time, to quit it:
Though we break up a fortnight, 'tis no matter.

SUBTLE
Who is it, Dol?

DOL
A fine young quodling.

FACE
O,
My lawyer's clerk, I lighted on, last night,
In Holborn, at the Dagger. He would have
(I told you of him) a familiar,
To rifle with, at horses, and win cups.

DOL
O, let him in.

SUBTLE
Stay. Who shall do't?

FACE
Get you
Your robes on. I will meet him, as going out.

DOL
And what shall I do?

FACE
Not be seen, away.
Seem you very reserved. [*Exit* DOL]

SUBTLE
Enough. [*Exit* SUBTLE]

177–9 *Common . . . Proper . . . Singular . . . Particular* grammatical categories used to indicate Dol's sexual range

178 *longest cut* they will draw straws for Dol

189 *quodling* an unripe apple; youth

191 *Dagger* the Dagger tavern was famous for pies and frumety. It was perhaps also a gambling house

192 *familiar* spirit

193 *rifle* gamble (raffle)

FACE God be w'you, sir.
I pray you, let him know that I was here.
His name is Dapper. I would gladly have stayed, but—

Act I, Scene ii

DAPPER [*within*]
Captain, I am here.
FACE Who's that? He's come, I think, Doctor.

[*Enter* DAPPER]

Good faith, sir, I was going away.
DAPPER In truth,
I am very sorry, Captain.
FACE But I thought
Sure, I should meet you.
DAPPER Ay, I am very glad.
I had a scurvy writ, or two, to make,
And I had lent my watch last night, to one
That dines, today, at the sheriff's: and so was robbed
Of my pass-time. [*Enter* SUBTLE *in doctor's robes*]
Is this the cunning-man?
FACE
This is his worship.
DAPPER Is he a Doctor?
DACE Yes.
DAPPER
And ha' you broke with him, Captain?
FACE Ay.
DAPPER And how?
FACE
Faith, he does make the matter, sir, so dainty,
I know not what to say—
DAPPER Not so, good Captain.
FACE
Would I were fairly rid on't, believe me.
DAPPER
Nay, now you grieve me, sir. Why should you wish so?
I dare assure you. I'll not be ungrateful.

6 *watch* a desirable status-commodity
10 *broke* broached the matter
11 *he does . . . dainty* he treats it with such fastidious caution

FACE
I cannot think you will, sir. But the law
Is such a thing—and then, he says, Read's matter
Falling so lately—
DAPPER Read? He was an ass,
And dealt, sir, with a fool.
FACE It was a clerk, sir.
DAPPER
A clerk?
FACE Nay, hear me, sir, you know the law
Better, I think—
DAPPER I should, sir, and the danger.
You know I showed the statute to you?
FACE You did so.
DAPPER
And will I tell, then? By this hand, of flesh,
Would it might never write good court-hand, more,
If I discover. What do you think of me,
That I am a *Chiause*?
FACE What's that?
DAPPER The Turk was, here—
As one would say, do you think I am a Turk?
FACE
I'll tell the Doctor so.
DAPPER Do, good sweet Captain.
FACE
Come, noble Doctor, 'pray thee, let's prevail,
This is the gentleman, and he is no *Chiause*.
SUBTLE
Captain, I have returned you all my answer.
I would do much, sir, for your love—but this
I neither may, nor can.

17 *Read's matter* in 1608 Simon Read, a Southwark doctor, was given a pardon for having (in November 1607) invoked three spirits in order to discover a thief
19 *a fool* presumably Tobias Matthews who had been robbed and called upon Read's assistance
22 *the statute* see I.i.112
24 *court-hand* a much abbreviated (and therefore hard to read) style of writing used in the law courts
25 *discover* reveal
26 *Chiause* in July 1607 a Turk named Mustafa arrived in England declaring himself ambassador from the Sultan, though he used only the title 'Chaush' (messenger). The Levant merchants were fooled into entertaining him at great cost and 'to play the Chaush . . . seems to have become a popular synonym for imposture'. *The Travels of Sir John Sanderson in the Levant*, ed. Sir W. Foster, London, 1931, p. xxxv

FACE
Tut, do not say so.
You deal, now, with a noble fellow, Doctor,
One that will thank you, richly, and he's no *Chiause*:
Let that, sir, move you.

SUBTLE
Pray you, forbear—

FACE
He has
Four angels, here—

SUBTLE
You do me wrong, good sir.

FACE
Doctor, wherein? To tempt you, with these spirits?

SUBTLE
To tempt my art, and love, sir, to my peril.
'Fore heaven, I scarce can think you are my friend,
That so would draw me to apparent danger.

FACE
I draw you? A horse draw you, and a halter,
You, and your flies together—

DAPPER
Nay, good Captain.

FACE
That know no difference of men.

SUBTLE
Good words, sir.

FACE
Good deeds, sir, Doctor Dogs-meat. 'Slight I bring you
No cheating Clim o' the Cloughs, or Claribels,
That look as big as five-and-fifty, and flush,
And spit out secrets, like hot custard—

DAPPER
Captain.

FACE
Nor any melancholic under-scribe,
Shall tell the Vicar: but, a special gentle,

45 *Dogs-meat* Dogges-mouth Q

---

37 *angels* gold coins bearing a picture of the Archangel Michael combatting a dragon. The word – conjoining the spiritual and the pecuniary – was much played upon, as here

38 *spirits* continues the play on 'angels'

42 *a horse draw you* i.e. in a cart to be hanged

46 *Clim o' the Cloughs . . . Claribels* Clim of the Clough, 'an archer good ynough' *(Ballad of Adam Bell)* and an outlaw. Nashe uses his name for the devil in *Pierce Pennilesse* (1592). Sir Claribel pursues the False Florimell in Spenser's *Faerie Queene* IV.ix

47 *as big as five-and-fifty, and flush* all 55 cards in the same suit – an unbeatable hand in Primero

50 *Vicar* vicar general, acting for the bishop in ecclesiastical courts
gentle gentleman

That is the heir to forty marks, a year,
Consorts with the small poets of the time,
Is the sole hope of his old grandmother,
That knows the law, and writes you six fair hands,
Is a fine clerk, and has his cyph'ring perfect,
Will take his oath, o' the Greek Testament
If need be, in his pocket: and can court
His mistress, out of Ovid.

DAPPER
Nay, dear Captain.

FACE
Did you not tell me, so?

DAPPER
Yes, but I'd ha' you
Use master Doctor, with some more respect.

FACE
Hang him proud stag, with his broad velvet head.
But, for your sake, I'd choke, ere I would change
An article of breath, with such a puck-fist—
Come let's be gone.

SUBTLE
Pray you, le' me speak with you.

DAPPER
His worship calls you, Captain.

FACE
I am sorry,
I e'er embarked myself, in such a business.

DAPPER
Nay, good sir. He did call you.

FACE
Will he take, then?

SUBTLE
First, hear me—

FACE
Not a syllable, 'less you take.

SUBTLE
Pray ye, sir—

56 *Testament* this is the Q reading; in F it is changed to 'Xenophon' which makes no sense except to highlight the absurdities to which censorship leads

---

54 *six fair hands* six styles of handwriting; probably those cited in John de Beau Chesne and John Baildon's *A Booke containing divers sortes of hands, as well the English as French secretarie with the Italian, Roman, Chancelry & Court hands*, London, 1571

55 *cyphering* book-keeping

58 *Ovid* if he courted out of the *Amores* he would be quite forward

61 *proud stag . . . velvet head* Subtle is wearing a doctor's velvet hat whose texture is like that of the plush on a stag's antlers

63 *puck-fist* puff-ball (i.e. wind-bag)

69 *assumpsit* legal term; lit. 'he has taken'; a voluntary, oral contract sealed with some form of payment

78 *blow up* ruin

FACE Upon no terms, but an *assumpsit.*
SUBTLE
Your humour must be law.

He takes the money

FACE Why now, sir, talk.
Now, I dare hear you with mine honour. Speak.
So may this gentleman too.
SUBTLE Why, sir—
FACE No whispering.
SUBTLE
'Fore heaven, you do not apprehend the loss
You do yourself, in this.
FACE Wherein? For what?
SUBTLE
Marry, to be so importunate for one,
That, when he has it, will undo you all:
He'll win up all the money i' the town.
FACE
How!
SUBTLE Yes. And blow up gamester, after gamester,
As they do crackers, in a puppet-play.
If I do give him a familiar,
Give you him all you play for; never set him:
For he will have it.
FACE You're mistaken, Doctor.
Why, he does ask one but for cups, and horses,
A rifling fly: none o' your great familiars.
DAPPER
Yes, Captain, I would have it, for all games.
SUBTLE
I told you so.
FACE 'Slight, that's a new business!
I understood you, a tame bird, to fly
Twice in a term, or so; on Friday nights,
When you had left the office: for a nag,
Of forty, or fifty shillings.
DAPPER Ay, 'tis true, sir,
But I do think, now, I shall leave the law,
And therefore—

69 *assumpsit* legal term; lit. 'he has taken'; a voluntary, oral contract sealed with some form of payment
78 *blow up* ruin
79 *crackers* fireworks
81 *set him* lay a wager with him
87 *I understood you* I thought you meant

FACE Why, this changes quite the case!
D'you think, that I dare move him?
DAPPER If you please, sir,
All's one to him, I see.
FACE What! For that money?
I cannot with my conscience. Nor should you
Make the request, methinks.
DAPPER No, sir, I mean
To add consideration.
FACE Why, then, sir,
I'll try. Say, that it were for all games, Doctor?
SUBTLE
I say, then, not a mouth shall eat for him
At any ordinary, but o' the score,
That is a gaming mouth, conceive me.
FACE Indeed!
SUBTLE
He'll draw you all the treasure of the realm,
If it be set him.
FACE Speak you this from art?
SUBTLE
Ay, sir, and reason too: the ground of art.
He's o' the only best complexion,
The Queen of Fairy loves.
FACE What! Is he!
SUBTLE Peace.
He'll overhear you. Sir, should she but see him—
FACE
What?
SUBTLE Do not you tell him.
FACE Will he win at cards too?
SUBTLE
The spirits of dead Holland, living Isaac,
You'd swear, were in him: such a vigorous luck
As cannot be resisted. 'Slight he'll put
Six o' your gallants, to a cloak, indeed.

97 *consideration* payment
99–100 *not a mouth . . . o' the score* because of him no gambler in town will be able to eat unless they chalk it up on the slate
100 *ordinary* eating house
103 *art* occult knowledge
109 *dead Holland, living Isaac* John and Isaac Holland were the first Dutch alchemists
111–12 *put . . . to a cloak* he'll reduce six gallants to nothing but their cloaks

FACE
A strange success, that some man shall be born to!
SUBTLE
He hears you, man—
DAPPER Sir, I'll not be ingrateful.
FACE
Faith, I have a confidence in his good nature:
You hear, he says, he will not be ingrateful.
SUBTLE
Why, as you please, my venture follows yours.
FACE
Troth, do it, Doctor. Think him trusty, and make him.
He may make us both happy in an hour:
Win some five thousand pound, and send us two on't.
DAPPER
Believe it, and I will, sir.
FACE And you shall, sir.
You have heard all?
DAPPER No, what was't? Nothing, I sir.

FACE *takes him aside*

FACE
Nothing?
DAPPER A little, sir.
FACE Well, a rare star
Reigned, at your birth.
DAPPER At mine, sir? No.
FACE The Doctor
Swears that you are—
SUBTLE Nay, Captain, you'll tell all, now.
FACE
Allied to the Queen of Fairy.
DAPPER Who? That I am?
Believe it, no such matter—
FACE Yes, and that
Yo' were born with a caul o' your head.
DAPPER Who says so?
FACE Come.
You know it well enough, though you dissemble it.

117 *my venture . . . yours* I'll risk it if you will
119 *happy* rich (the Latin *beatus* translates as both)
128 *born with a caul* a sign of good luck

DAPPER
I'fac, I do not. You are mistaken.
FACE
How!
Swear by your fac? And in a thing so known
Unto the Doctor? How shall we, sir, trust you
I' the other matter? Can we ever think,
When you have won five, or six thousand pound,
You'll send us shares in't, by this rate?
DAPPER
By Jove, sir,
I'll win ten thousand pound, and send you half.
I'fac's no oath.
SUBTLE
No, no, he did but jest.
FACE
Go to. Go, thank the Doctor, He's your friend
To take it so.
DAPPER
I thank his worship.
FACE
So?
Another angel.
DAPPER
Must I?
FACE
Must you? 'Slight,
What else is thanks? Will you be trivial?
[*Gives money* to SUBTLE]
Doctor,
When must he come, for his familiar?
DAPPER
Shall I not ha' it with me?
SUBTLE
O, good sir!
There must a world of ceremonies pass,
You must be bathed, and fumigated, first;
Besides, the Queen of Fairy does not rise,
Till it be noon.
FACE
Not, if she danced, tonight.
SUBTLE
And she must bless it.
FACE
Did you never see
Her royal Grace, yet?
DAPPER
Whom?
FACE
Your aunt of Fairy?
SUBTLE
Not, since she kissed him, in the cradle, Captain,

135 *Jove* Gad Q
137 *fac's* fac is Q
138 *He's* He is Q

---

130 *I'fac* in faith
141 *trivial* petty
147 *tonight* last night

I can resolve you that.

FACE Well, see her Grace,
Whate'er it cost you, for a thing that I know!
It will be somewhat hard to compass: but,
How ever, see her. You are made, believe it,
If you can see her. Her Grace is a lone woman,
And very rich, and if she take a fancy,
She will do strange things. See her, at any hand.
'Slid, she may hap to leave you all she has!
It is the Doctor's fear.

DAPPER How will't be done, then?

FACE
Let me alone, take you no thought. Do you
But say to me, Captain, I'll see her Grace.

DAPPER
Captain, I'll see her Grace.

FACE Enough. *One knocks without*

SUBTLE Who's there?
Anon. [*To* FACE] (Conduct him forth, by the back way.)
Sir, against one o'clock, prepare yourself.
Till when you must be fasting; only, take
Three drops of vinegar, in, at your nose;
Two at your mouth; and one, at either ear;
Then, bathe your fingers' ends; and wash your eyes;
To sharpen your five senses; and, cry *hum*,
Thrice; and then *buz*, as often; and then, come.

FACE
Can you remember this?

DAPPER I warrant you.

FACE
Well, then, away. 'Tis, but your bestowing
Some twenty nobles, 'mong her Grace's servants;
And, put on a clean shirt: you do not know
What grace her Grace may do you in clean linen.
[*Exeunt*]

151 *resolve you that* answer that for you
152 *for* on account of
174 *clean shirt* fairies are traditionally particular about cleanliness

Act I, Scene iii

[*Enter*] SUBTLE

SUBTLE [*To* DRUGGER]
Come in. [*He turns and calls out*]
(Good wives, I pray you forbear me, now.
Troth I can do you no good, till afternoon.)

[*Enter* DRUGGER]

What is your name, say you, Abel Drugger?
DRUGGER Yes, sir.
SUBTLE
A seller of tobacco?
DRUGGER Yes, sir.
SUBTLE 'Umh.
Free of the Grocers?
DRUGGER Ay, and't please you.
SUBTLE Well—
Your business, Abel?
DRUGGER This, and't please your worship,
I am a young beginner, and am building
Of a new shop, and't like your worship; just,
At corner of a street: (here's the plot on't.)
And I would know, by art, sir, of your worship,
Which way I should make my door, by necromancy.
And, where my shelves. And, which should be for boxes.
And, which for pots. I would be glad to thrive, sir.
And, I was wished to your worship, by a gentleman,
One Captain Face, that says you know men's planets,
And their good angels, and their bad.
SUBTLE I do,
If I do see 'em—

[*Enter* FACE]

FACE What! My honest Abel?
Thou art well met, here!

1 *Good wives* this is addressed to some putative clients outside
5 *Free of the grocers* a member of the Grocers' guild or company
9 *plot* groundplan
14 *wished to* recommended

DRUGGER
Troth, sir, I was speaking,
Just, as your worship came here, of your worship.
I pray you, speak for me to master Doctor.

FACE
He shall do anything. Doctor, do you hear?
This is my friend, Abel, an honest fellow,
He lets me have good tobacco, and he does not
Sophisticate it, with sack-lees, or oil,
Nor washes it in muscadel, and grains,
Nor buries it, in gravel, under ground,
Wrapped up in greasy leather, or pissed clouts:
But keeps it in fine lily-pots, that opened,
Smell like conserve of roses, or French beans.
He has his maple block, his silver tongs,
Winchester pipes, and fire of juniper.
A neat, spruce-honest-fellow, and no gold-smith.

SUBTLE
He's a fortunate fellow, that I am sure on—

FACE
Already, sir, ha' you found it? Lo' thee Abel!

SUBTLE
And, in right way toward riches—

FACE
Sir.

SUBTLE
This summer,
He will be of the clothing of his company:
And, next spring, called to the scarlet. Spend what he can.

24 *Sophisticate . . . oil* William Barclay records, 'Some . . . haue *Tabacco* from *Florida* indeede, but because either it is exhausted of spiritualitie, or the radicall humor is spent, and wasted, or it hath gotten moysture by the way, or it hath been dried for expedition in the Sunne, or carried too negligently, they sophisticate and farde the same in sundrie sortes with blacke spice, *Galanga, aqua vitae*, Spanish wine, Anise seeds, oyle of Spicke and such like. ' *Nepenthes, or the vertues of Tabacco*, Edinburgh, 1614, A4v–A5

25 *muscadel* a fragrant white wine
grains spice

27 *pissed clouts* rags dampened with urine

30–1 *maple block . . . silver tongs, Winchester pipes . . . fire of juniper* the maple block is for shredding the tobacco leaf; the silver tongs for holding hot coals; Winchester made famously good tobacco pipes; the fire of Juniper wood (very long-burning) enables customers to light their pipes in Abel's shop which, typically, is arranged for the consumption, as well as purchase, of tobacco

32 *gold-smith* usurer

36 *of the clothing of his company* i.e. Drugger will be made a livery-man of his company. Each of the trade guilds and companies had a distinctive livery

37 *called to the scarlet* be made a sherriff

FACE
What, and so little beard?
SUBTLE
Sir, you must think,
He may have a receipt, to make hair come.
But he'll be wise, preserve his youth, and fine for't:
His fortune looks for him, another way.
FACE
'Slid, Doctor, how canst thou know this so soon?
I am amused at that!
SUBTLE
By a rule, Captain,
In metoposcopy, which I do work by,
A certain star i'the forehead, which you see not.
Your chestnut, or your olive-coloured face
Does never fail: and your long ear doth promise.
I knew't, by certain spots too, in his teeth,
And on the nail of his mercurial finger.
FACE
Which finger's that?
SUBTLE
His little finger. Look.
Y'were born upon a Wednesday?
DRUGGER
Yes, indeed, sir.
SUBTLE
The thumb, in chiromanty, we give Venus;
The forefinger to Jove; the midst, to Saturn;
The ring to Sol; the least, to Mercury:
Who was the lord, sir, of his horoscope,
His house of life being Libra, which foreshowed,
He should be a merchant, and should trade with balance.

38 *and so little beard?* and so young?
40 *fine for't H.&S.* read this as meaning 'pay the fine for refusing office'; but it may simply mean 'and be fine because of it'
43 *amused* amazed; bewildered
44 *metoposcopy* the art of reading character from physiognomy
46–7 *Your chestnut . . . fail* 'The colours of the Body, and especially of the face denote the Humour and inclination of the person . . . Those that be chestnut or olive colour are Jovialists and honest people, open without painting or cheating', R. Sanders, *Physionomie and Chiromancie, Metoposcopie*, London, 1653, pp. 166–7
48 *mercurial finger* the little finger; each finger is assigned a separate planet in J. B. Porta's *Coelestis Physiognomoniae*, Naples, 1603, lib. v, cap. xiii
52 *chiromanty* palmistry
54–7 *the least . . . balance* Libra is ruled, not by Mercury, but by Venus. But Mercury is a more encouraging ruling planet for the aspiring business man. (Jonson's own sign, Gemini, is ruled by Mercury)
57 *trade with balance* the scales are the sign of Libra

FACE
Why, this is strange! Is't not, honest Nab?
SUBTLE
There is a ship now, coming from Ormus,
That shall yield him, such a commodity
Of drugs—[*looking at plan*]
this is the west, and this the south?
DRUGGER
Yes, sir.
SUBTLE And those are your two sides?
DRUGGER Ay, sir.
SUBTLE
Make me your door, then, south; your broad side, west:
And, on the east side of your shop, aloft,
Write *Mathlai*, *Tarmiel*, and *Baraborat*;
Upon the north part, *Rael*, *Velel*, *Thiel*.
They are the names of those mercurial spirits,
That do fright flies from boxes.
DRUGGER Yes, sir.
SUBTLE And
Beneath your threshold, bury me a loadstone
To draw in gallants, that wear spurs: the rest,
They'll seem to follow.
FACE That's a secret, Nab!
SUBTLE
And, on your stall, a puppet, with a vice,
And a court-fucus, to call city-dames.
You shall deal much, with minerals.
DRUGGER Sir, I have,
At home, already—
SUBTLE Ay, I know, you have arsenic,

67 *mercurial* Mercurian Q

59 *Ormus* Hormuz on the Persian Gulf, source of much spice
65–6 *Mathlai* . . . . *Thiel* quoted from the *Heptameron, seu Elementa magica Pietri Abano Philosophi* (appended to Cornelius Agrippa's *De Occulta Philosophia*, Paris?, no date)
68 *fright flies from boxes* protect your stores from flies
69 *loadstone* magnet
71 *seem* be seen (a Latinism, *videri*)
72 *vice* wire mechanism for operating the puppet
73 *fucus* cosmetic; one used at court would be desirable to socially-aspiring city women

Vitriol, sal-tartar, argaile, alkali,
Cinoper: I know all. This fellow, Captain,
Will come, in time, to be a great distiller,
And give a say (I will not say directly,
But very fair) at the philosopher's stone.

FACE
Why, how now, Abel! Is this true?

DRUGGER
Good Captain,
What must I give?

FACE
Nay, I'll not counsel thee.
Thou hear'st, what wealth (he says, spend what thou canst)
Th'art like to come to.

DRUGGER
I would gi' him a crown.

FACE
A crown! And toward such a fortune? Heart,
Thou shalt rather gi' him thy shop. No gold about thee?

DRUGGER
Yes, I have a portague, I ha' kept this half year.

FACE
Out on thee, Nab; 'Slight, there was such an offer—
'Shalt keep't no longer, I'll gi'it him for thee?
Doctor, Nab prays your worship, to drink this:
[*Gives money to* SUBTLE]
and swears
He will appear more grateful, as your skill
Does raise him in the world.

DRUGGER
I would entreat
Another favour of his worship.

FACE
What is't, Nab?

DRUGGER
But, to look over, sir, my almanack,
And cross out my ill days, that I may neither
Bargain, nor trust upon them.

FACE
That he shall, Nab.
Leave it, it shall be done, 'gainst afternoon.

76 *Vitriol* sulphuric acid
sal-tartar carbonate of potash
argaile cream of tartar
alkali caustic soda
77 *Cinoper* red mercuric sulphide
79 *give a say* make a try for
87 *portague* a Portuguese gold coin
95 *ill days* days that are astrologically inauspicious
97 *'gainst* by

SUBTLE
And a direction for his shelves.

FACE
Now, Nab?
Art thou well pleased, Nab?

DRUGGER
Thank, sir, both your worships.

FACE
Away.

[*Exit* DRUGGER]

Why, now, you smoky persecutor of nature!
Now, do you see, that something's to be done,
Beside your beech-coal, and your corsive waters,
Your crosslets, crucibles, and cucurbites?
You must have stuff, brought home to you, to work on?
And, yet, you think, I am at no expense,
In searching out these veins, then following 'em,
Then trying 'em out. 'Fore God, my intelligence
Costs me more money, than my share oft comes to,
In these rare works.

SUBTLE
You are pleasant, sir.

[*Enter*] DOL

How now?

Act I, Scene iv

FACE
What says, my dainty Dolkin?

DOL
Yonder fish-wife
Will not away. And there's your giantess,
The bawd of Lambeth.

SUBTLE
Heart, I cannot speak with 'em.

DOL
Not, afore night, I have told 'em, in a voice,
Thorough the trunk, like one of your familiars.
But I have spied Sir Epicure Mammon—

SUBTLE
Where?

DOL
Coming along, at the far end of the lane,
Slow of his feet, but earnest of his tongue,

102 *beech-coal* beech wood made the best charcoal
corsive corrosive
103 *crosslets* melting pots
cucurbites gourd-shaped retorts used in distillation
107 *intelligence* information
3 *Lambeth* noted for prostitutes and thieves
5 *Thorough the trunk* i.e. through a speaking tube

To one, that's with him.

SUBTLE
Face, go you, and shift.
[*Exit* FACE]
Dol, you must presently make ready too—

DOL
Why, what's the matter?

SUBTLE
O, I did look for him
With the sun's rising: marvel, he could sleep!
This is the day, I am to perfect for him
The *magisterium*, our great work, the stone;
And yield it, made, into his hands: of which,
He has, this month, talked, as he were possessed.
And, now, he's dealing pieces on't, away.
Methinks, I see him, entering ordinaries,
Dispensing for the pox; and plaguey-houses,
Reaching his dose; walking Moorfields for lepers;
And offering citizens' wives pomander-bracelets,
As his preservative, made of the elixir;
Searching the spittle, to make old bawds young;
And the highways, for beggars, to make rich:
I see no end of his labours. He will make
Nature ashamed of her long sleep: when art,
Who's but a step-dame, shall do more, than she,
In her best love to mankind, ever could.
If his dream last, he'll turn the age, to gold. [*Exeunt*]

Act II, Scene i

[*Enter*] MAMMON, SURLY

MAMMON
Come on, sir. Now, you set your foot on shore

16 *possessed* possess'd on't Q

9 *shift* change
14 *magisterium* master work
17 *dealing... away* giving parts of it away (in imagination)
20 *Reaching* offering
Moorfields a stretch of reclaimed marshland which in Jonson's time was being laid out in parks. It was noted for beggars, and lepers were allowed to beg there
21 *pomander-bracelets* a pomander was a perfumed ball carried as a protection against infection (and smells)
23 *spittle* hospital
27 *step-dame* the debate as to the respective roles of Art and Nature was a commonplace. See, e.g., *The Winter's Tale*, IV.iv.79–102

In *novo orbe*; here's the rich Peru:
And there within, sir, are the golden mines,
Great Solomon's Ophir! He was sailing to't,
Three years, but we have reached it in ten months.
This is the day, wherein, to all my friends,
I will pronounce the happy word, be rich.
This day, you shall be *spectatissimi*.
You shall no more deal with the hollow die,
Or the frail card. No more be at charge of keeping
The livery-punk, for the young heir, that must
Seal, at all hours, in his shirt. No more
If he deny, ha' him beaten to't, as he is
That brings him the commodity. No more
Shall thirst of satin, or the covetous hunger
Of velvet entrails, for a rude-spun cloak,
To be displayed at Madam Augusta's, make
The sons of sword, and hazard fall before
The golden calf, and on their knees, whole nights,

11 *the young* my yong Q

1–5 *Now, you set your foot . . . ten months* Mammon is promising Surly a 'new world' of wealth. The discovery of the Americas by Renaissance voyagers became a potent metaphor for much non-topographical experience of the time. Solomon was believed to have possessed the Philosopher's Stone and to have fetched his wealth 'once in three years' from Ophir (*I Kings* x.22)

2 *novo orbe* the new world; i.e. America; both a metaphor for wealth and its source (through imports)
Peru synonym for great wealth; the location of El Dorado

8 *spectatissimi* (Lat.) very much regarded

9 *hollow die* loaded dice (hollowed and then weighted with lead)

10–14 *No more . . . commodity* an allusion to the 'commodity swindle' (described in Greene's *Defence of Coney-Catching*, *The Works of Robert Greene*, ed. A. B. Grosart, London 1881–6, vol. xi, p. 53) by which a borrower was constrained to take all or part of a loan in the form of often unsaleable goods (see III.iv.87–99). The 'livery-punk' is a prostitute ('livery' implies that she is part of the regular retinue) who, by compromising the young heir in *déshabille*, furthers the money-lender's attempts to make him 'seal' such an unprofitable bargain

16 *velvet entrails* velvet linings. The contemporary fashion for 'slashing' the top layer of fabric to allow the contrasting inner stuff to show through could be disturbingly reminiscent of gaping wounds. See Lovelace's 'La Bella Bona Roba' 'whose white-sattin upper coat of skin/[Is] Cut upon velvet rich incarnadin'

17 *Madam Augusta* presumably a brothel madam

18 *The sons of sword, and hazard* thugs and gamblers

19 *golden calf* a false idol (*Exodus* xxxii)

Commit idolatory with wine, and trumpets:
Or go a-feasting, after drum and ensign.
No more of this. You shall start up young viceroys,
And have your punks, and punketees, my Surly.
And unto thee, I speak it first, be rich.
Where is my Subtle, there? Within ho?

FACE *Within* Sir.
He'll come to you, by and by.

MAMMON That's his fire-drake,
His lungs, his Zephyrus, he that puffs his coals,
Till he firk nature up, in her own centre.
You are not faithful, sir. This night, I'll change
All, that is metal, in thy house, to gold.
And, early in the morning, will I send
To all the plumbers, and the pewterers,
And buy their tin, and lead up: and to Lothbury,
For all the copper.

SURLY What, and turn that too?

MAMMON
Yes, and I'll purchase Devonshire, and Cornwall,
And make them perfect Indies! You admire now?

SURLY
No faith.

MAMMON But when you see th'effects of the great med'cine!
Of which one part projected on a hundred
Of Mercury, or Venus, or the Moon,
Shall turn it, to as many of the Sun;

30 *thy* my Q (the F reading may be an error)

---

22 *start up* generate
23 *punketees* little whores
26 *fire-drake* firey dragon or meteor; here used figuratively for fire-maker
27 *lungs* bellows; i.e. assistant
Zephyrus the west wind personified
28 *firk* stir
29 *faithful* trusting
33 *Lothbury* 'This streete is possessed for the most part by Founders, that cast Candlestickes, Chafingdishes, Spice mortars and such like Copper or Laton workes.' John Stow, *A Survey of London*, ed. C. L. Kingsford, Oxford, 1908, p. 277
35 *Devonshire, and Cornwall* the site of tin and copper mines
36 *perfect Indies* the West Indies, thought to be rich in 'spice and mine' (Donne, 'The Sun Rising')
admire are struck
39–40 *Mercury . . . the sun* Mercury is quicksilver; Venus stands for copper, the moon for silver and the sun for gold

Nay, to a thousand, so *ad infinitum*:
You will believe me.

SURLY
Yes, when I see't, I will.
But, if my eyes do cozen me so (and I
Giving 'em no occasion) sure, I'll have
A whore, shall piss 'em out, next day.

MAMMON
Ha! Why?
Do you think, I fable with you? I assure you,
He that has once the flower of the sun,
The perfect ruby, which we call elixir,
Not only can do that, but by its virtue,
Can confer honour, love respect, long life,
Give safety, valour: yea, and victory,
To whom he will. In eight, and twenty days,
I'll make an old man, of fourscore, a child.

SURLY
No doubt, he's that already.

MAMMON
Nay, I mean,
Restore his years, renew him, like an eagle,
To the fifth age; make him get sons, and daughters,
Young giants; as our philosophers have done
(The ancient patriarchs afore the flood)
But taking, once a week, on a knife's point,
The quantity of a grain of mustard, of it:
Become stout Marses, and beget young Cupids.

SURLY
The decayed Vestals of Pict-Hatch would thank you,
That keep the fire alive, there.

MAMMON
'Tis the secret
Of nature, naturized 'gainst all infections,

47–8 *flower of the sun . . . perfect ruby . . . elixir* all synonyms for the Philosopher's Stone

55 *like an eagle* 'Thy youth is renewed like the eagle's', *Psalms* ciii.5

56 *the fifth age* 'The *fifth* age, named *Mature Manhood*, hath . . . fifteen yeares of continuance, and therefore makes his progress so far as six and fifty yeares' (quoted from *The Treasury of Ancient and Modern Times*, 1613, by Malone on *As You Like It*, II.vii.151)

58 *ancient patriarchs* the longevity of the Patriarchs was attributed to their knowledge of alchemy

62 *The decayed Vestals of Pict-Hatch* Pict-Hatch (just south of where Goswell Road and Old Street now meet) was a haunt of prostitutes. Vestals were traditionally virgin temple servers. The fire maintained by these vestals is presumably that of venereal infection

64 *nature, naturized* scholastic philosophy distinguished between creating nature *(natura naturans)* and created nature *(natura naturata)*. The stone is part of creat*ed* nature

Cures all diseases, coming of all causes,
A month's grief, in a day; a year's, in twelve:
And, of what age soever, in a month.
Past all the doses, of your drugging Doctors.
I'll undertake, withal, to fright the plague
Out o' the kingdom, in three months.

SURLY
And I'll
Be bound, the players shall sing your praises, then,
Without their poets.

MAMMON
Sir, I'll do't. Meantime,
I'll give away so much, unto my man,
Shall serve th' whole city, with preservative,
Weekly, each house his dose, and at the rate—

SURLY
As he that built the waterwork, does with water?

MAMMON
You are incredulous.

SURLY
Faith, I have a humour,
I would not willingly be gulled. Your stone
Cannot transmute me.

MAMMON
Pertinax, Surly,
Will you believe antiquity? Records?
I'll show you a book, where Moses, and his sister,
And Solomon have written, of the art;
Ay, and a treatise penned by Adam.

SURLY
How!

MAMMON
O' the philosopher's stone, and in High Dutch.

SURLY
Did Adam write, sir, in High Dutch?

MAMMON
He did:
Which proves it was the primitive tongue.

71–2 *the players . . . poets* the London theatres were closed while the plague was rife because they were thought to be places of infection and also to invite infection as retribution for the immorality they housed. The players would sing Mammon's praises if they found themselves in work again

76 *the waterwork* probably the pump-house built by Bevis Bulmer at Broken Wharf in 1594. This supplied Cheapside and Fleet Street with water from the Thames

77 *I have a humour* it is my temperament

81–3 *Moses . . . Adam* Mammon is not alone in his attribution of alchemical lore to Moses, Solomon and Adam. See *H.&S.* for references

84 *High Dutch* hoch Deutsch (high German); Joannes Goropius Becanus, a Flemish physician, claimed that German was the original language and that the early Germans were not at the Tower of Babel. He declared this in a treatise called *Hermathena* (c. 1580)

SURLY
What paper?

MAMMON
On cedar board.

SURLY
O that, indeed (they say)
Will last 'gainst worms.

MAMMON
'Tis like your Irish wood,
'Gainst cobwebs. I have a piece of Jason's fleece, too,
Which was no other, than a book of alchemy,
Writ in large sheepskin, a good fat ram-vellum.
Such was Pythagoras' thigh, Pandora's tub;
And, all that fable of Medea's charms,
The manner of our work: the bulls, our furnace,
Still breathing fire; our *argent-vive*, the dragon;
The dragon's teeth, mercury sublimate,
That keeps the whiteness, hardness, and the biting;
And they are gathered, into Jason's helm,
(Th' alembic) and then sowed in Mars his field,
And, thence, sublimed so often, till they are fixed.
Both this, th' Hesperian garden, Cadmus' story,
Jove's shower, the boon of Midas, Argus' eyes,

87–9 *cedar board . . . Irish wood* cedar wood was known for its durability, Irish wood for its ability to repel spiders and insects

89 *Jason's fleece* 'Cornelius *Agrippa* maketh mention of some Philosophers that held the skinne of the sheepe that bare the golden fleece, to be nothing but a booke of Alcumy written vpon it' *The Works of Thomas Nashe*, ed. R. B. McKerrow, Oxford, 1966, iii, 221

92 *Pythagoras' thigh* supposedly golden (*Diogenes Laertius*, viii.i). Martin Delrio associates both this and Pandora's box *(tub)* with alchemy in his *Disquisitiones Magicae*, 1599

93–100 *that fable . . . are fixed* in order to gain the golden fleece Jason had to yoke and plough with two brazen-footed, fire-breathing bulls. He then had to sow dragons' teeth which sprang up as armed warriors. Medea, his witch-lover, taught him how to cope

95 *argent-vive* quicksilver

96 *mercury sublimate* chloride of mercury – a corrosive (hence the 'biting')

99 *alembic* distilling apparatus

Mars his field an old genitive form (=Mars' field) Mars stands for iron

101 *th' Hesperian garden* site of golden apples guarded by a dragon

101 *Cadmus' story* Cadmus founded Thebes on the spot where he killed a dragon, then planted its teeth which sprang up as warriors. All but five of these warriors killed each other

102 *Jove's shower* Jove entered Danae as a shower of gold

the boon of Midas Bacchus gave Midas the dubious gift of turning all he touched to gold

Argus' eyes Argus was a dog with a hundred eyes whom Juno set to guard the woman-heifer Io whom her husband, Jupiter, loved

Boccace his Demogorgon, thousands more,
All abstract riddles of our stone. How now?

Act II, Scene ii

[*Enter*] FACE [*dressed as bellows-man to them*]

MAMMON
Do we succeed? Is our day come? And holds it?
FACE
The evening will set red, upon you, sir;
You have colour for it, crimson: the red ferment
Has done his office. Three hours hence, prepare you
To see projection.
MAMMON Pertinax, my Surly,
Again, I say to thee, aloud: be rich.
This day, thou shalt have ingots: and, tomorrow,
Give lords th'affront. Is it, my Zephyrus, right?
Blushes the bolt's head?
FACE Like a wench with child, sir,
That were, but now, discovered to her master.
MAMMON
Excellent witty Lungs! My only care is,
Where to get stuff, enough now, to project on,
This town will not half serve me.
FACE No, sir? Buy
The covering off o' churches.
MAMMON That's true.
FACE Yes.
Let 'em stand bare, as do their auditory.
Or cap 'em, new, with shingles.

13 *Buy* Take Q

---

103 *Boccace his Demogorgon* a primeval god named by Boccaccio in his *Genealogica Deorum*. Demogorgon is also mentioned by Milton and Spenser
104 *abstract riddles* allegories
3 *red ferment* 'Red is last in the work of *Alkimy*', Norton, *Ordinal*, in *T.C.B.*, p. 56; 'ferment' is leaven
8 *Give lords th'affront* look lords in the eye as their equal
9 *bolt's head* 'a globular flask with a long cylindrical neck' (*OED*); it 'blushes' as it reddens
15 *auditory* congregation (who remove their hats)
16 *shingles* slats of wood used like roof tiles

MAMMON No, good thatch:
Thatch will lie light upo' the rafters, Lungs.
Lungs, I will manumit thee, from the furnace;
I will restore thee thy complexion, Puff,
Lost in the embers; and repair this brain,
Hurt wi' the fume o' the metals.

FACE I have blown, sir,
Hard, for your worship; thrown by many a coal,
When 'twas not beech; weighed those I put in, just,
To keep your heat still even; these bleared eyes
Have waked, to read your several colours, sir,
Of the pale citron, the green lion, the crow,
The peacock's tail, the plumed swan.

MAMMON And, lastly,
Thou hast descried the flower, the *sanguis agni*?

FACE
Yes, sir.

MAMMON Where's master?

FACE At's prayers, sir, he,
Good man, he's doing his devotions,
For the success.

MAMMON Lungs, I will set a period,
To all thy labours: thou shalt be the master
Of my seraglio.

FACE Good, sir.

MAMMON But do you hear?
I'll geld you, Lungs.

FACE Yes, sir.

MAMMON For I do mean
To have a list of wives, and concubines,
Equal with Solomon; who had the stone

33 *seraglio* seraglia Q, F

---

18 *manumit* release

22 *when 'twas not beech* in Lyly's *Gallathea* the alchemist says 'I may have onely Beechen coales' II.ii.78

26–7 *pale citron . . . swan* each of these items names a colour and stage in the alchemical process: 'Pale, and Black, wyth falce Citryne, unparfyt Whyte & Red, Pekoks fethers in color gay, the Raynbow whych shall overgoe/The Spottyd Panther wyth the Lyon greene, the Crowys byll bloe as lede;/These shall appere before the parfyt Whyte', Ripley, *Compound of Alchymie*, in *T.C.B.*, p. 188

28 *sanguis agni* 'blood of the lamb' (Lat.); a red indicating successful projection. The term has Christian, sacrificial connotations

33 *seraglio* harem

Alike, with me: and I will make me, a back
With the elixir, that shall be as tough
As Hercules, to encounter fifty a night.
Th'art sure, thou saw'st it blood?

FACE
Both blood, and spirit, sir.

MAMMON
I will have all my beds, blown up; not stuffed:
Down is too hard. And then, mine oval room,
Filled with such pictures, as Tiberius took
From Elephantis: and dull Aretine
But coldly imitated. Then, my glasses,
Cut in more subtle angles, to disperse,
And multiply the figures, as I walk
Naked between my *succubae*. My mists
I'll have of perfume, vapoured 'bout the room,
To lose ourselves in; and my baths, like pits
To fall into: from whence, we will come forth,
And roll us dry in gossamer, and roses.
(Is it arrived at ruby?) – Where I spy
A wealthy citizen, or rich lawyer,
Have a sublimed pure wife, unto that fellow
I'll send a thousand pound, to be my cuckold.

FACE
And I shall carry it?

MAMMON
No. I'll ha' no bawds,
But fathers, and mothers. They will do it best.
Best of all others. And, my flatterers
Shall be the pure, and gravest of Divines,
That I can get for money. My mere fools,
Eloquent burgesses, and then my poets,
The same that writ so subtly of the fart,

58 *They will . . . all others* not in Q
60 *pure* best Q

---

41 *beds, blown up* Lampridius, *Elagabalus*, xxv
43–4 Suetonius, *Tiberius*, cap. xliii
44 *Aretine* Pietro Aretino (1492–1550); Italian poet whose *Sonnetti Lussuriosi* (1523) illustrated by Giulio Romano were notorious erotica of their time
45 *glasses* Seneca, *Naturales Quaestiones*, I.xvi, refers to Hostius Quadra's use of mirrors to arouse himself
48 *succubae* demons assuming female form in order to have sexual intercourse with humans
60 *the pure, and gravest* purest and gravest
62 *burgesses* members of Parliament
63 *that writ . . . of the fart* perhaps the anonymous author of 'The fart Censured in the Parliament House' – a ballad commemorating an event in 1607. But Jonson himself wrote much of farts in 'The Famous Voyage'

Whom I will entertain, still, for that subject.
The few, that would give out themselves, to be
Court, and town stallions, and, eachwhere, belie
Ladies, who are known most innocent, for them;
Those will I beg, to make me eunuchs of:
And they shall fan me with ten ostrich tails
Apiece, made in a plume, to gather wind.
We will be brave, Puff, now we ha' the med'cine.
My meat, shall all come in, in Indian shells,
Dishes of agate, set in gold, and studded,
With emeralds, sapphires, hyacinths, and rubies.
The tongues of carps, dormice, and camels' heels,
Boiled i' the spirit of Sol, and dissolved pearl,
(Apicius' diet, 'gainst the epilepsy)
And I will eat these broths, with spoons of amber,
Headed with diamant, and carbuncle.
My footboy shall eat pheasants, calvered salmons,
Knots, godwits, lampreys: I myself will have
The beards of barbels, served, instead of salads;
Oiled mushrooms; and the swelling unctuous paps
Of a fat pregnant sow, newly cut off,
Dressed with an exquisite, and poignant sauce;
For which, I'll say unto my cook, there's gold,
Go forth, and be a knight.

FACE Sir, I'll go look
A little, how it heightens.

MAMMON Do. [*Exit* FACE]
My shirts
I'll have of taffeta-sarsnet, soft, and light
As cobwebs; and for all my other raiment

74 *hyacinths* not the flowers but precious blue stones
75 *tongues of carps* 'The tongues of *Carps* are noted to be choice and costly meat', Isaac Walton, *The Compleat Angler* (1653), Oxford, 1935, p. 149
dormice the Romans ate them (Apicius gives a recipe), and the practice has lately been revived in England by a firm hoping to catch the novelty delicacy market
camels' heels Lampridius, *Elagabalus*, xx, tells how this emperor ate these 'in imitation of Apicius'—he also ate the beards of mullets
77 *Apicius* the Roman author of *Artis Magiricae* (The Art of Cooking)
80 *calvered* a culinary process only applicable to fresh firm fish
81 *Knots* a species of snipe
godwits marsh birds, similar to curlews
lampreys eel-shaped fish
82 *barbels* a species of carp with fleshy filaments hanging from its mouth. See note to line 75
85 *poignant* piquant
89 *taffeta-sarsnet* a fine soft silk

It shall be such, as might provoke the Persian;
Were he to teach the world riot, anew.
My gloves of fishes', and birds' skins, perfumed
With gums of paradise, and eastern air—

SURLY
And do you think to have the stone, with this?

MAMMON
No, I do think, t' have all this, with the stone.

SURLY
Why, I have heard, he must be *homo frugi*,
A pious, holy, and religious man,
One free from mortal sin, a very virgin.

MAMMON
That makes it, sir, he is so. But I buy it.
My venture brings it me. He, honest wretch,
A notable, superstitious, good soul,
Has worn his knees bare, and his slippers bald,
With prayer, and fasting for it: and, sir, let him
Do it alone, for me, still. Here he comes,
Not a profane word, afore him: 'tis poison.

Act II, Scene iii

[*Enter*] SUBTLE [*to them*]

MAMMON
Good morrow, Father.

SUBTLE
Gentle son, good morrow,
And, to your friend, there. What is he, is with you?

MAMMON
An heretic, that I did bring along,
In hope, sir, to convert him.

SUBTLE
Son, I doubt
You're covetous, that thus you meet your time
I' the just point: prevent your day, at morning.

91 *the Persian* Sardanapalus, king of Ninevah 9 B.C. – of legendary luxury

94 *gums of paradise* incense from the middle East (where the Garden of Eden had supposedly been)

97–9 *homo frugi . . . virgin* piety, purity and a lack of material ambition are prerequisite to alchemical success

4 *doubt* fear

6 *I' the just point* punctually, on the dot
prevent anticipate

This argues something, worthy of a fear
Of importune, and carnal appetite.
Take heed, you do not cause the blessing leave you,
With your ungoverned haste. I should be sorry,
To see my labours, now, e'en at perfection,
Got by long watching, and large patience,
Not prosper, where my love, and zeal hath placed 'em.
Which (heaven I call to witness, with yourself,
To whom, I have poured my thoughts) in all my ends,
Have looked no way, but unto public good,
To pious uses, and dear charity,
Now grown a prodigy with men. Wherein
If you, my son, should now prevaricate,
And, to your own particular lusts, employ
So great, and catholic a bliss: be sure,
A curse will follow, yea, and overtake
Your subtle, and most secret ways.

MAMMON
I know, sir,
You shall not need to fear me. I but come,
To ha' you confute this gentleman.

SURLY
Who is,
Indeed, sir, somewhat costive of belief
Toward your stone: would not be gulled.

SUBTLE
Well, son,
All that I can convince him in, is this,
The work is done: bright Sol is in his robe.
We have a med'cine of the triple soul,
The glorified spirit. Thanks be to heaven,
And make us worthy of it. Ulen Spiegel.

18 *Now* No Q, F
25 SURLY SVB. Q

---

12 *watching* waking
19 *prevaricate* walk crookedly (Lat. *praevaricari*)
21 *catholic* general (as opposed to 'particular', line 20)
29 *bright Sol is in his robe* Sol (the sun), the planet governing gold, is ready to officiate
30 *triple soul* according to scholastic thought there are three kinds of soul: the vegetable (capable of growth), the animal (capable of reproduction) and the intellectual (capable of thought). Humans are possessed of all three and are linked to the angels by their intellectual souls
32 *Ulen Spiegel* lit. 'Owl-glass'; Til Eulen Spiegel is the hero of several German jest books. He is a practical joker. William Copeland's *Howle glass* was published in England between 1548 and 1560

FACE
[*within*] Anon, sir.

[*Enter* FACE]

SUBTLE
Look well to the register,
And let your heat, still, lessen by degrees,
To the aludels.

FACE
Yes, sir.

SUBTLE
Did you look
O' the bolt's head yet?

FACE
Which, on D, sir?

SUBTLE
Ay.
What's the complexion?

FACE
Whitish.

SUBTLE
Infuse vinegar,
To draw his volatile substance, and his tincture:
And let the water in glass E be filtered,
And put into the gripe's egg. Lute him well;
And leave him closed in *balneo*.

FACE
I will, sir.

[*Exit* FACE]

SURLY
What a brave language here is? Next to canting?

SUBTLE
I have another work; you never saw, son,
That, three days since, passed the philosopher's wheel,
In the lent heat of Athanor; and's become
Sulphur o' nature.

MAMMON
But 'tis for me?

SUBTLE
What need you?

33 *register* a contrivance – usually consisting of moveable metal plates – for regulating the passage of air, heat and smoke
35 *aludels* pear-shaped vessels, open at either end; used for sublimation
36 *on D* Face gives the impression of a number of different operations going on concurrently, each distinguished by a letter of the alphabet
37 *complexion* colour
38, 40 *his . . . him* the use of the personal pronoun is in keeping with the alchemists' belief that all matter is animate
40 *gripe's egg* an egg-shaped pot (a 'gripe' is a vulture)
Lute stop up the gaps with lute (clay)
41 *in balneo* in a bath (of boiling water or hot sand)
42 *canting* cant was the private (though much publicised) language of thieves
44 *philosopher's wheel* alchemical cycle
45 *lent* slow (Lat.)
Athanor a 'digesting furnace' maintaining a low, constant heat
46 *Sulphur o' nature* pure sulphur in an immutable state

You have enough in that is perfect.

MAMMON
O, but—

SUBTLE
Why, this is covetise!

MAMMON
No, I assure you,
I shall employ it all, in pious uses,
Founding of colleges, and grammar schools,
Marrying young virgins, building hospitals,
And now, and then, a church.

[*Enter* FACE]

SUBTLE
How now?

FACE
Sir, please you,
Shall I not change the filter?

SUBTLE
Marry, yes.
And bring me the complexion of glass B.

[*Exit* FACE]

MAMMON
Ha' you another?

SUBTLE
Yes, son, were I assured
Your piety were firm, we would not want
The means to glorify it. But I hope the best:
I mean to tinct C in sand-heat, tomorrow,
And give him imbibition.

MAMMON
Of white oil?

SUBTLE
No, sir, of red. F is come over the helm too,
I thank my Maker, in S. Mary's bath,
And shows *lac virginis*. Blessed be heaven.
I sent you of his faeces there, calcined.
Out of that calx, I ha' won the salt of mercury.

MAMMON
By pouring on your rectified water?

58 *sand-heat* i.e. in a sand bath
59 *imbibition* steeping in liquid
59–60 *white . . . red* mercury is 'white', sulphur 'red'; the oils would be derivatives of these
61 *S. Mary's bath* the 'bain Marie' of modern cooking
62 *lac virginis* 'Mercurial Water, the Dragon's Tail: it washes and coagulates without any manual labour' Ruland, *A Lexicon of Alchemy*, Frankfurt, 1612
63 *faeces* sediment
calcined reduced to a powder having had its humidity drawn out by heat
64 *calx* the powdery result of calcining
salt oxide
65 *rectified* distilled

SUBTLE
Yes, and reverberating in Athanor.

[*Enter* FACE]

How now? What colour says it?
FACE
The ground black, sir.
MAMMON
That's your crow's head?
SURLY
Your cockscomb's, is't not?
SUBTLE
No, 'tis not perfect, would it were the crow.
That work wants something.
SURLY
(O, I looked for this.
The hay is a-pitching.)
SUBTLE
Are you sure, you loosed 'em
I' their own menstrue?
FACE
Yes, sir, and then married 'em,
And put 'em in a bolt's head, nipped to digestion,
According as you bade me; when I set
The liquor of Mars to circulation,
In the same heat.
SUBTLE
The process, then, was right.
FACE
Yes, by the token, sir, the retort broke,
And what was saved, was put into the pelican,
And signed with Hermes' seal.
SUBTLE
I think 'twas so.
We should have a new amalgama.
SURLY
(O, this ferret
Is rank as any pole-cat.)

66 *reverberating* being heated by reflected heat
68 *crow's head* blackness resulting from calcination
71 *The hay is a-pitching* a 'hay' is a net 'pitched' or set in front of rabbits' burrows. The metaphor is from the language of coney-catching
71–2 *loosed . . . menstrue* dissolved them in the fluid distilled from them
73 *nipped* sealed
digestion slow extraction of soluble substances through 'cooking' in a digesting oven
75 *liquor of Mars* molten iron
78 *pelican* an alembic with a tubular head and two curved spouts, each of which re-enter the vessel (like a pelican wounding its own breast)
79 *signed with Hermes' seal* hermetically sealed
80 *amalgama* mixture of metals with mercury
80–1 *ferret . . . pole-cat* the images sustain the coney-catching metaphor; pole-cats are smellier than ferrets

SUBTLE But I care not.
Let him e'en die; we have enough beside,
In embrion. H has his white shirt on?
FACE Yes, sir,
He's ripe for inceration: he stands warm,
In his ash-fire. I would not, you should let
Any die now, if I might counsel, sir,
For luck's sake to the rest. It is not good.
MAMMON
He says right.
SURLY (Ay, are you bolted?)
FACE Nay, I know't, sir,
I have seen th' ill fortune. What is some three ounces
Of fresh materials?
MAMMON Is't no more?
FACE No more, sir,
Of gold, t'amalgam, with some six of mercury.
MAMMON
Away, here's money. What will serve?
FACE Ask him, sir.
MAMMON
How much?
SUBTLE Give him nine pound: you may gi' him ten.
SURLY
Yes, twenty, and be cozened, do.
MAMMON There 'tis.
SUBTLE
This needs not. But that you will have it, so,
To see conclusions of all. For two
Of our inferior works, are at fixation.
A third is in ascension. Go your ways.
Ha' you set the oil of Luna in kemia?
FACE
Yes, sir.
SUBTLE And the philosopher's vinegar?
FACE Ay. [*Exit* FACE]

83 *in embrion* in their early stages
83 *has his white shirt on* has turned white
84 *inceration* bringing the substances to the consistency of soft wax
88 *bolted* entered the snare (another coney-catching image)
97 *fixation* the process of reducing a volatile substance to a stable form
99 *oil of Luna* white elixir
kemia from the Greek *χυμέια*: alchemy; here it probably implies entrance into the whole process
100 *philosopher's vinegar* either mercury or a corrosive vinegar made of mead

SURLY
We shall have a salad.
MAMMON When do you make projection?
SUBTLE
Son, be not hasty. I exalt our med'cine,
By hanging him in *balneo vaporoso*;
And giving him solution; then congeal him;
And then dissolve him; then again congeal him;
For look, how oft I iterate the work,
So many times, I add unto his virtue.
As, if at first, one ounce convert a hundred,
After his second loose, he'll turn a thousand;
His third solution, ten; his fourth, a hundred.
After his fifth, a thousand thousand ounces
Of any imperfect metal, into pure
Silver, or gold, in all examinations,
As good, as any of the natural mine.
Get you your stuff here, against afternoon,
Your brass, your pewter, and your andirons.
MAMMON
Not those of iron?
SUBTLE Yes, you may bring them, too.
We'll change all metals.
SURLY I believe you, in that.
MAMMON
Then I may send my spits?
SUBTLE Yes, and your racks.
SURLY
And dripping pans, and pot-hangers, and hooks?
Shall he not?
SUBTLE If he please.
SURLY To be an ass.
SUBTLE
How, sir!
MAMMON This gent'man, you must bear withal.
I told you, he had no faith.

101 *salad* a salad dressing from the oil and vinegar; the term was actually used by alchemists

103 *balneo vaporoso* a contrivance for suspending vessels in steam

106–7 *how oft . . . virtue* the potency of the stone is increased each time I subject it to the process of dissolution and congelation

108 *convert* turn into

109 *loose* dissolution

116 *andirons* metal supports for logs in a fire; fire-dogs

SURLY And little hope, sir,
But, much less charity, should I gull my self.

SUBTLE
Why, what have you observed, sir, in our art,
Seems so impossible?

SURLY But your whole work, no more.
That you should hatch gold in a furnace, sir,
As they do eggs, in Egypt!

SUBTLE Sir, do you
Believe that eggs are hatched so?

SURLY If I should?

SUBTLE
Why, I think that the greater miracle.
No egg, but differs from a chicken, more,
Than metals in themselves.

SURLY That cannot be.
The egg's ordained by nature, to that end:
And is a chicken in *potentia*.

SUBTLE
The same we say of lead, and other metals,
Which would be gold, if they had time.

MAMMON And that
Our art doth further.

SUBTLE Ay, for 'twere absurd
To think that nature, in the earth, bred gold
Perfect, i' the instant. Something went before.
There must be remote matter.

SURLY Ay, what is that?

SUBTLE
Marry, we say—

MAMMON Ay, now it heats: stand Father.
Pound him to dust—

SUBTLE It is, of the one part,
A humid exhalation, which we call
Materia liquida, or the unctuous water;
On th' other part, a certain crass, and viscous

123–4 *faith . . . hope . . . charity* the Cardinal Virtues and all necessary to alchemical success

128 *eggs, in Egypt* Pliny mentions eggs hatching on dung-hills in Egypt (*Nat. Hist.*, x.lxxv.153)

131–76 *No egg . . . metals* Subtle's argument is taken, in places almost verbatim, from Martin Delrio's *Disquisitiones Magicae*, 1599

140 *remote matter* the first matter

144 *unctuous* oily

145 *crass* dense

Portion of earth; both which, concorporate,
Do make the elementary matter of gold:
Which is not, yet, *propria materia*,
But common to all metals, and all stones.
For, where it is forsaken of that moisture
And hath more dryness, it becomes a stone;
Where it retains more of the humid fatness,
It turns to sulphur, or to quicksilver:
Who are the parents of all other metals.
Nor can this remote matter, suddenly,
Progress so from extreme, unto extreme,
As to grow gold, and leap o'er all the means.
Nature doth, first, beget th' imperfect; then
Proceeds she to the perfect. Of that airy,
And oily water, mercury is engendered;
Sulphur o' the fat, and earthy part: the one
(Which is the last) supplying the place of male,
The other of the female, in all metals.
Some do believe hermaphrodeity,
That both do act, and suffer. But, these two
Make the rest ductile, malleable, extensive.
And, even in gold, they are; for we do find
Seeds of them, by our fire, and gold in them:
And can produce the species of each metal
More perfect thence, than nature doth in earth.
Beside, who doth not see, in daily practice,
Art can beget bees, hornets, beetles, wasps,
Out of the carcasses, and dung of creatures;
Yea, scorpions, of an herb, being ritely placed:
And these are living creatures, far more perfect,
And excellent, than metals.

MAMMON Well said, Father!
Nay, if he take you in hand, sir, with an argument,

176 *metals* metall Q

---

146 *concorporate* fused into a single body
148 *propria materia* a specific substance
165 *do act, and suffer* are active and passive; this division of all things into active and passive, male and female, light and dark, accords with the ancient Chinese divisions of Yang and Yin
166 *extensive* able to be stretched out
169 *species* essence or form
172–3 *Art . . . creatures* this was widely believed
174 *ritely placed* Delrio has 'rite posita': 'placed in accordance with the rites'; an audience would only hear 'rightly'. The herb is basil

He'll bray you in a mortar.

SURLY Pray you, sir, stay.
Rather, than I'll be brayed, sir, I'll believe,
That alchemy is a pretty kind of game,
Somewhat like tricks o' the cards, to cheat a man,
With charming.

SUBTLE Sir?

SURLY What else are all your terms,
Whereon no one o' your writers 'grees with other?
Of your elixir, your *lac virginis*,
Your stone, your med'cine, and your chrysosperm,
Your sal, your sulphur, and your mercury,
Your oil of height, your tree of life, your blood,
Your marcasite, your tutty, your magnesia,
Your toad, your crow, your dragon, and your panther,
Your sun, your moon, your firmament, your adrop,
Your lato, azoch, zernich, chibrit, heautarit,
And then, your red man, and your white woman,
With all your broths, your menstrues, and materials,
Of piss, and eggshells, women's terms, man's blood,
Hair o' the head, burnt clouts, chalk, merds, and clay,
Powder of bones, scalings of iron, glass,
And worlds of other strange ingredients,
Would burst a man to name?

178 *bray* pound
182–207 *What else . . . allegories* also from Delrio
185 *chrysosperm* seed of gold
187 *tree of life* Philosopher's Stone
blood redness
188 *marcasite* crystalised iron pirites
tutty impure zinc oxide (collected from chimneys)
189 *toad . . . crow . . . panther* all colours which appear at different stages of the work; the dragon is mercury
190 *firmament* blue
adrop lead
191 *lato* latten; a compound similar to brass
azoch mercury (Arabic *az-zaug*)
zernich trisulphide of arsenic
chibrit sulphur
heautarit mercury
194 *eggshells* according to Aubrey, John Dee 'used to distill Egge-shells, and 'twas from hence that Ben. Johnson had his hint of the *Alkimist*, whom he meant.' *Brief Lives*, ed. O. L. Dick, Harmondsworth, 1972, p. 249
women's terms menstrual blood
195 *clouts* rags
merds faeces

SUBTLE And all these, named
Intending but one thing: which art our writers
Used to obscure their art.
MAMMON Sir, so I told him,
Because the simple idiot should not learn it,
And make it vulgar.
SUBTLE Was not all the knowledge
Of the Egyptians writ in mystic symbols?
Speak not the Scriptures, oft, in parables?
Are not the choicest fables of the poets,
That were the fountains, and first springs of wisdom,
Wrapped in perplexed allegories?
MAMMON I urged that,
And cleared to him, that Sisyphus was damned
To roll the ceaseless stone, only, because
He would have made ours common.

DOL *is seen*

Who is this?
SUBTLE
God's precious – What do you mean? Go in, good lady,
Let me entreat you.

[*Exit* DOL]

Where's this varlet?

[*Enter* FACE]

FACE Sir?
SUBTLE
You very knave! Do you use me, thus?
FACE Wherein, sir?
SUBTLE
Go in, and see, you traitor. Go.

[*Exit* FACE]

MAMMON Who is it, sir?
SUBTLE
Nothing, sir. Nothing.
MAMMON What's the matter? Good, sir!
I have not seen you thus distempered. Who is 't?
SUBTLE
All arts have still had, sir, their adversaries,

201–7 *simple idiot . . . allegories* cf. Henry Reynolds on the rationale of hieroglyphs, 'that high and Mysticall matters should by riddles and enigmaticall knotts be kept inuiolate from the prophane Multitude', *Mythomystes* in *Critical Essays of the Seventeenth Century*, ed. J. E. Spingarn, Oxford, 1957, vol. I, p. 156

208 *Sisyphus* condemned to an eternity of rolling a boulder up a hill in Hades; the boulder always rolls back when the summit is reached

210 *common* this word punningly cues in Dol

But ours the most ignorant.

FACE *returns*

What now?

FACE
'Twas not my fault, sir, she would speak with you.

SUBTLE
Would she, sir? Follow me. [*Exit* SUBTLE]

MAMMON Stay, Lungs.

FACE I dare not, sir.

MAMMON
Stay man, what is she?

FACE A lord's sister, sir.

MAMMON
How! Pray thee stay?

FACE She's mad, sir, and sent hither—
(He'll be mad too.

MAMMON I warrant thee.) Why sent hither?

FACE
Sir, to be cured.

SUBTLE [*within*] Why, rascal!

FACE Lo you. Here, sir.

He goes out

MAMMON
'Fore God, a Bradamante, a brave piece.

SURLY
Heart, this is a bawdy-house! I'll be burnt else.

MAMMON
O, by this light, no. Do not wrong him. He's
Too scrupulous, that way. It is his vice.
No, he's a rare physician, do him right.
An excellent Paracelsian! And has done
Strange cures with mineral physic. He deals all
With spirits, he. He will not hear a word
Of Galen, or his tedious recipes.

[*Enter*] FACE *again*

How now, Lungs!

FACE Softly, sir, speak softly. I meant
To ha' told your worship all. This must not hear.

MAMMON
No, he will not be gulled; let him alone.

221–2 Q transposed in F

---

225 *Bradamante* a woman knight in Ariosto's *Orlando Furioso*

230 *Paracelsian* a follower of Paracelsus (1493–1541) whose holistic medical theories involved the application of chemical principles. He was believed to have learned the secret of the Philosopher's Stone while in Constantinople

FACE
You're very right, sir, she is a most rare scholar;
And is gone mad, with studying Broughton's works.
If you but name a word, touching the Hebrew,
She falls into her fit, and will discourse
So learnedly of genealogies,
As you would run mad, too, to hear her, sir.

MAMMON
How might one do t'have conference with her, Lungs?

FACE
O, divers have run mad upon the conference.
I do not know, sir: I am sent in haste,
To fetch a vial.

SURLY
Be not gulled, Sir Mammon.

MAMMON
Wherein? Pray ye, be patient.

SURLY
Yes, as you are.
And trust confederate knaves, and bawds, and whores.

MAMMON
You are too foul, believe it. Come here, Ulen.
One word.

FACE
I dare not, in good faith.

MAMMON
Stay, knave.

FACE
He's extreme angry, that you saw her, sir.

MAMMON
[*Gives money*] Drink that. What is she, when she's out of her fit?

FACE
O, the most affablest creature, sir! So merry!
So pleasant! She'll mount you up, like quicksilver,
Over the helm; and circulate, like oil,
A very vegetal: discourse of state,
Of mathematics, bawdry, anything—

MAMMON
Is she no way accessible? No means,

249 *Ulen* Zephyrus Q

---

238 *Broughton* Hugh Broughton (1549–1612), a puritan and rabbinical scholar. His idiolect is referred to in *Volpone*: SIR POL. Is not his language rare? PER. But alchemy,/I never heard the like – or Broughton's books. (II.ii.118–20)

241 *genealogies* Broughton attempted to settle Old Testament chronology in *A Concent of Scripture*, 1590, from which Dol quotes in IV.v

255 *helm* see II.i.98; the head of the penis is also implied

256 *vegetal* see I.i.39; here the emphasis is on Dol's liveliness

No trick, to give a man a taste of her – wit—
Or so? Ulen!

FACE I'll come to you again, sir. [*Exit* FACE]

MAMMON
Surly, I did not think, one o' your breeding
Would traduce personages of worth.

SURLY Sir Epicure,
Your friend to use: yet, still, loth to be gulled.
I do not like your philosophical bawds.
Their stone is lechery enough, to pay for,
Without this bait.

MAMMON 'Heart, you abuse yourself.
I know the lady, and her friends, and means,
The original of this disaster. Her brother
Has told me all.

SURLY And yet, you ne'er saw her
Till now?

MAMMON O, yes, but I forgot. I have (believe it)
One of the treacherous'st memories, I do think,
Of all mankind.

SURLY What call you her, brother?

MAMMON My lord—
He wi' not have his name known, now I think on't.

SURLY
A very treacherous memory!

MAMMON O' my faith—

SURLY
Tut, if you ha' it not about you, pass it,
Till we meet next.

MAMMON Nay, by this hand, 'tis true.
He's one I honour, and my noble friend,
And I respect his house.

SURLY Heart! Can it be,
That a grave sir, a rich, that has no need,
A wise sir, too, at other times, should thus
With his own oaths, and arguments, make hard means
To gull himself? And, this be your elixir,

259 *her-wit-/Or so* her-/Wit? or so Q
260 *Ulen* not in Q
272 SURLY SVB. Q, F

---

268 *original* source
275 *pass it* leave it

Your *lapis mineralis*, and your lunary,
Give me your honest trick, yet, at primero,
Or gleek; and take your *lutum sapientis*,
Your *menstruum simplex*: I'll have gold, before you,
And, with less danger of the quicksilver;
Or the hot sulphur.

[*Enter* FACE]

FACE *to* SURLY Here's one from Captain Face, sir,
Desires you meet him i' the Temple Church,
Some half hour hence, and upon earnest business.

He whispers MAMMON

Sir, if you please to quit us, now; and come,
Again, within two hours: you shall have
My master busy examining o' the works;
And I will steal you in, unto the party,
That you may see her converse. [*To* SURLY] Sir, shall
I say,
You'll meet the Captain's worship?

SURLY Sir, I will.
(But, by attorney, and to a second purpose.
Now, I am sure, it is a bawdy house;
I'll swear it, were the Marshal here, to thank me:
The naming this Commander, doth confirm it.
Don Face! Why, he's the most authentic dealer
I' these commodities! The Superintendent
To all the quainter traffickers, in town.
He is their Visitor, and does appoint
Who lies with whom; and at what hour; what price;

283 *lapis mineralis* mineral stone
lunary the plant now known as honesty; in alchemy this would be associated with the moon's metal, silver
284 *primero* a card game; the best hand of four cards is the 'prime'
285 *gleek* a card game for three players
lutum sapientis 'the philosopher's lute' – a quick-drying paste used to seal vessels quickly
286 *menstruum simplex* simple solvent
287–8 *less danger ... sulphur* quicksilver was used in the treatment of venereal disease which Surly suggests Mammon is likely to contract in this place; sulphur is a remedy for skin infections
289 *Temple Church* the official church for law students and – like St. Paul's – a centre for gossip and meetings
295 *converse* the word has a sexual sense
297 *by attorney* not in my own person
303 *quainter traffickers* prostitutes; 'quaint' used to mean cunt

Which gown; and in what smock; what fall; what tire.
Him, will I prove, by a third person, to find
The subleties of this dark labyrinth:
Which, if I do discover, dear Sir Mammon,
You'll give your poor friend leave, though no philosopher,
To laugh: for you that are, 'tis thought, shall weep.)

FACE
Sir. He does pray, you'll not forget.

SURLY
I will not, sir.
Sir Epicure, I shall leave you?

MAMMON
I follow you, straight.
[*Exit* SURLY]

FACE
But do so, good sir, to avoid suspicion.
This gent'man has a parlous head.

MAMMON
But wilt thou, Ulen,
Be constant to thy promise?

FACE
As my life, sir.

MAMMON
And wilt thou insinuate what I am? And praise me?
And say I am a noble fellow?

FACE
O, what else, sir?
And, that you'll make her royal, with the stone,
An Empress; and yourself King of Bantam.

MAMMON
Wilt thou do this?

FACE
Will I, sir?

MAMMON
Lungs, my Lungs!
I love thee.

FACE
Send your stuff, sir, that my master
May busy himself, about projection.

MAMMON
Th'hast witched me, rogue: take, [*Gives money*] go.

FACE
Your jack, and all, sir.

315 *Ulen* not in Q

---

306 *fall* falling band or veil
307 *prove* test (Lat. *probare*)
315 *parlous* difficult to deal with, risky, cunning
320 *Bantam* a city in north Java, once capital of a Mohammetan empire and legendary for its magnificence
324 *jack* a machine for turning a spit (driven by weights)

MAMMON
Thou art a villian – I will send my jack;
And the weights too. Slave, I could bite thine ear.
Away, thou dost not care for me.
FACE
Not I, sir?
MAMMON
Come, I was born to make thee, my good weasel;
Set thee on a bench: and, ha' thee twirl a chain
With the best lord's vermin, of 'em all.
FACE
Away, sir.
MAMMON
A Count, nay, a Count Palatine—
FACE
Good sir, go.
MAMMON
—Shall not advance thee, better: no, nor faster.
[*Exit* MAMMON]

Act II, Scene iv

[*Enter*] SUBTLE, DOL [*to* FACE]

SUBTLE
Has he bit? Has he bit?
FACE
And swallowed too, my Subtle.
I ha' given him line, and now he plays, i' faith.
SUBTLE
And shall we twitch him?
FACE
Thorough both the gills.
A wench is a rare bait, with which a man
No sooner's taken, but he straight firks mad.
SUBTLE
Dol, my Lord Whats'hum's sister, you must now
Bear yourself statelich.
DOL
O, let me alone.
I'll not forget my race, I warrant you.
I'll keep my distance, laugh, and talk aloud;
Have all the tricks of a proud scurvy lady,
And be as rude's her woman.

331 *Count Palatine* originally a count attached to an imperial palace with supreme judicial authority; later, a count permitted supreme jurisdiction of his province
2 *line . . . plays* the image is from angling
5 *firks mad* falls into transports of madness
7 *statelich* in a stately way (Dutch, or German – hence the script); the Netherlands wars, in which Jonson served, brought many such words into England

FACE
Well said, Sanguine.

SUBTLE
But will he send his andirons?

FACE
His jack too;
And's iron shoeing-horn: I ha' spoke to him. Well,
I must not lose my wary gamester, yonder.

SUBTLE
O Monsieur Caution, that will not be gulled?

FACE
Ay, if I can strike a fine hook into him, now,
The Temple Church, there I have cast mine angle.
Well, pray for me. I'll about it.

One knocks

SUBTLE
What, more gudgeons!
Dol, scout, scout; stay Face, you must go to the door:
Pray God, it be my Anabaptist. Who is't, Dol?

DOL [*At window*]
I know him not. He looks like a gold-end-man.

SUBTLE
Gods so! 'Tis he, he said he would send. What call you him?
The sanctified Elder, that should deal
For Mammon's jack, and andirons! Let him in.
Stay, help me off, first, with my gown. Away
Madam, to your withdrawing chamber. [*Exit* DOL]
Now,
In a new tune, new gesture, but old language.
This fellow is sent, from one negotiates with me
About the stone, too; for the holy Brethren
Of Amsterdam, the exiled Saints: that hope
To raise their discipline, by it. I must use him
In some strange fashion, now, to make him admire me.

11 *Sanguine* those in whom the sanguine (bloody) humour is predominant are optimistic, bold and amorous

17 *angle* fishing line

18 *gudgeons* small, freshwater fish, used as bait but themselves easily caught

20 *Anabaptist* member of the non-conformist sect of Anabaptists who advocated adult baptism, community of goods and no authority other than the Scriptures. They originated on the Continent in the 1520s and began to arrive in England in the 1530s (in 1535 a proclamation against their heresy was issued)

21 *gold-end-man* a buyer and seller of old gold

29–30 *holy Brethren . . . Saints* the Anabaptists attempted to take control of several Dutch cities, including Amsterdam; they fled to England to escape the consequent persecutions

Act II, Scene v

[*Enter*] ANANIAS [*to them*]

SUBTLE
Where is my drudge?
FACE
Sir.
SUBTLE
Take away the recipient,
And rectify your menstrue, from the phlegma.
Then pour it, o' the Sol, in the cucurbite,
And let 'em macerate, together.
FACE
Yes, sir.
And save the ground?
SUBTLE
No. *Terra damnata*
Must not have entrance, in the work. Who are you?
ANANIAS
A faithful Brother, if it please you.
SUBTLE
What's that?
A Lullianist? A Ripley? *Filius artis*?
Can you sublime, and dulcify? Calcine?
Know you the *sapor pontic*? *Sapor styptic*?
Or, what is homogene, or heterogene?
ANANIAS
I understand no heathen language, truly.

10 *styptick* stipstick Q, F

---

2 *phlegma* watery distillate
4 *macerate* soften by soaking
5 *the ground* the sediment which remains after distillation
Terra damnata damned earth
8 *Lullianist* follower of Raymond Lull (1235–1315), Spanish missionary, deviser of mnemonic schemes and (reputedly) alchemist; many alchemical works are attributed to him
Ripley follower of George Ripley (d. *c.* 1490), author of *The Compound of Alchemy* (in *T.C.B.*); he did much to popularise in England works attributed to Lull
Filius artis a 'son of the art' (Lat.); Subtle pretends to misunderstand Ananias' description of himself as 'A faithful Brother'
9 *dulcify* sweeten by dissolving the salt from a substance
10 *sapor pontic . . . Sapor styptic* nine 'sapors' (tastes) were distinguished by alchemists; five are created by heat and four (including pontic and stiptic) by cold

SUBTLE
Heathen, you Knipper-Doling? Is *Ars sacra*,
Or *chrysopoeia*, or *spagyrica*,
Or the pamphysic, or panarchic knowledge,
A heathen language?

ANANIAS Heathen Greek, I take it.

SUBTLE
How? Heathen Greek?

ANANIAS All's heathen, but the Hebrew.

all that's not originary is heathen ~~does~~ absurd, but & doesn't play represent nothing but fallen language

SUBTLE
Sirrah, my varlet, stand you forth, and speak to him
Like a philosopher: answer, i' the language.
Name the vexations, and the martyrizations
Of metals, in the work.

FACE Sir, Putrefaction,
Solution, Ablution, Sublimation,
Cohobation, Calcination, Ceration, and
Fixation.

SUBTLE This is heathen Greek, to you, now?
And when comes Vivification?

FACE After Mortification.

SUBTLE
What's Cohobation?

FACE 'Tis the pouring on

13 *Knipper-Doling* Bernard Knipperdollinck was a leading Anabaptist and instrumental in the occupation of Münster in 1534 where the Anabaptists established a 'Kingdom of God' under the rule of John of Leyden
Ars sacra the sacred art
14 *chrysopoeia* gold-making (Greek)
spagyrica a word supposedly coined by Paracelsus from the Greek σπαω (to stretch and rend) and αγειρω (to collect together); it signifies the Paracelsian method of alchemy by separation and combination
15 *pamphysic, or panarchic knowledge* knowledge of all nature or all power
17 *All's heathen, but the Hebrew* Hebrew was believed by some to be the unfallen language that Adam first used
19 *i' the language* in the language of alchemy
20 *vexations* contortions
martyrizations various processes of reduction to which the metals are subjected; the metaphor suits the hearer
21 *Putrefaction* breaking down
Ablution washing
23 *Cohobation* repeated distillation
Ceration see II.iii.84
25 *Vivification* the process of extracting a pure substance from a compound
Mortification breaking down of substance

Your *Aqua Regis*, and then drawing him off,
To the trine circle of the seven spheres.

SUBTLE
What's the proper passion of metals?

FACE
Malleation.

SUBTLE
What's your *ultimum supplicium auri*?

FACE
Antimonium.

SUBTLE
This 's heathen Greek, to you? And, what's your mercury?

FACE
A very fugitive, he will be gone, sir.

SUBTLE
How know you him?

FACE
By his viscosity,
His oleosity, and his suscitability.

SUBTLE
How do you sublime him?

FACE
With the calce of eggshells,
White marble, talc.

SUBTLE
Your *magisterium*, now?
What's that?

FACE
Shifting, sir, your elements,
Dry into cold, cold into moist, moist in –
To hot, hot into dry.

SUBTLE
This 's heathen Greek to you, still?
Your *lapis philosophicus*?

FACE
'Tis a stone, and not

27 *Aqua Regis* 'King's Water'; a mixture of vitriol and hydrochloric acid; it is so named because it is able to dissolve the 'noble' metals

28 *the trine circle of the seven spheres:* 'Know, too, that no solution will take place in your electrum unless it thrice runs perfectly through the sphere of seven planets'. *The Hermetic and Alchemical Writings of Paracelsus*, ed. A. E. Waite, 2 vols, London 1894, vol. ii, p. 105

29 *passion* again, the religious dimension of this word fits it to the hearer

30 *ultimum supplicium auri* extreme punishment for gold
Antimonium antimony – a slight alloy which destroys the malleability of gold

34 *oleosity* oiliness
suscitability excitability

35 *calce* calx (i.e. powder)

37–9 *Shifting* . . . *dry* F. H. Mares (in the Revels edition of the play) suggests that this may be the 'philosopher's wheel' of II.iii.44. The process involves placing substances into their opposing elements in order to reduce them to their essences

A stone; a spirit, a soul, and a body:
Which, if you do dissolve, it is dissolved,
If you coagulate, it is coagulated,
If you make it to fly, it flieth.

SUBTLE Enough.

[*Exit* FACE]

This 's heathen Greek, to you? What are you, sir?

ANANIAS
Please you, a servant of the exiled Brethren,
That deal with widows' and with orphans' goods;
And make a just account, unto the Saints:
A Deacon.

SUBTLE O, you are sent from master Wholesome,
Your teacher?

ANANIAS From Tribulation Wholesome,
Our very zealous Pastor.

SUBTLE Good. I have
Some orphans' goods to come here.

ANANIAS Of what kind, sir?

SUBTLE
Pewter, and brass, andirons, and kitchen ware,
Metals, that we must use our med'cine on:
Wherein the Brethren may have a penn'orth,
For ready money.

ANANIAS Were the orphans' parents
Sincere professors?

SUBTLE Why do you ask?

ANANIAS Because
We then are to deal justly, and give (in truth)
Their utmost value.

SUBTLE 'Slid, you'd cozen, else,
And, if their parents were not of the faithful?
I will not trust you, now I think on 't,
Till I ha' talked with your Pastor. Ha' you brought money
To buy more coals?

ANANIAS No, surely.

SUBTLE No? How so?

ANANIAS
The Brethren bid me say unto you, sir.
Surely, they will not venture any more,

48 *Saints* Ananias is anticipating the mass canonization of the brethren
57 *professors* of the Anabaptist faith

Till they may see projection.

SUBTLE
How!

ANANIAS
You've had,
For the instruments, as bricks, and loam, and glasses,
Already thirty pound; and, for materials,
They say, some ninety more: and, they have heard, since,
That one, at Heidelberg, made it, of an egg,
And a small paper of pin-dust.

SUBTLE
What's your name?

ANANIAS
My name is Ananias.

SUBTLE
Out, the varlet
That cozened the Apostles! Hence, away,
Flee Mischief; had your holy Consistory
No name to send me, of another sound;
Than wicked Ananias? Send your Elders,
Hither, to make atonement for you, quickly.
And gi' me satisfaction; or out goes
The fire: and down th' alembics, and the furnace,
Piger Henricus, or what not. Thou wretch,
Both Sericon, and Bufo, shall be lost,
Tell 'em. All hope of rooting out the Bishops,
Or th' Antichristian Hierarchy shall perish,
If they stay threescore minutes. The Aqueity,
Terreity, and Sulphureity
Shall run together again, and all be annulled,
Thou wicked Ananias.

[*Exit* ANANIAS]

This will fetch 'em,
And make 'em haste towards their gulling more.
A man must deal like a rough nurse, and fright
Those, that are froward, to an appetite.

70 *Heidelberg* believed to be the centre of alchemy

71 *pin-dust* metallic dust produced in the manufacture of pins (Germany was ahead of England in this; pins were not produced in England until 1626)

72–3 *Ananias . . . Apostles* see *Acts* v 1–11

74 *Consistory* assembly

76 *Elders* high-ranking church officers

80 *Piger Henricus* a 'lazy Henry': a multiple furnace fired by a single, central fire

81 *Sericon, and Bufo* red and black tincture ('Bufo' is 'the toad')

82–3 *All hope . . . Hierarchy* many saw the retention of bishops in the Church of England as a residue of popery

84–6 *The Aqueity . . . annulled* all the work of separation and purification will be undone

90 *froward* hard to please

Act II, Scene vi

[*Enter*] DRUGGER, FACE [*dressed as Captain to* SUBTLE]

FACE
He's busy with his spirits, but we'll upon him.
SUBTLE
How now! What mates? What Bayards ha' we here?
FACE
I told you, he would be furious. Sir, here's Nab,
Has brought you another piece of gold, to look on:
[*To* DRUGGER] (We must appease him. Give it me) and prays you,
You would devise (what is it Nab?)
DRUGGER A sign, sir.
FACE
Ay, a good lucky one, a thriving sign, Doctor.
SUBTLE
I was devising now.
FACE [*To* SUBTLE] ('Slight, do not say so,
He will repent he ga' you any more.)
What say you to his constellation, Doctor?
The Balance?
SUBTLE No, that way is stale, and common.
A townsman, born in Taurus, gives the bull;
Or the bull's head: in Aries, the ram.
A poor device. No, I will have his name
Formed in some mystic character; whose radii,
Striking the senses of the passers-by,
Shall, by a virtual influence, breed affections,
That may result upon the party owns it:
As thus—
FACE Nab!

2 *Bayards* Bayard was a common name for a horse (see Chaucer, *Troilus and Criseyde* I, 218
11 *Balance* Libra
12 *gives* uses as his sign
15 *radii* emanations
17 *virtual influence* influence of its power
affections inclinations

SUBTLE He first shall have a bell, that's Abel;
And, by it, standing one, whose name is Dee,
In a rug gown; there's D and Rug, that's Drug:
And, right anenst him, a dog snarling *Er*;
There's Drugger, Abel Drugger. That's his sign.
And here's now mystery, and hieroglyphic.

FACE
Abel, thou art made.

DRUGGER Sir, I do thank his worship. [*Bows*]

FACE
Six o' thy legs more, will not do it, Nab.
He has brought you a pipe of tobacco, Doctor.

DRUGGER Yes, sir:
I have another thing, I would impart—

FACE
Out with it, Nab.

DRUGGER Sir, there is lodged, hard by me,
A rich young widow—

FACE Good! A *bona roba*?

DRUGGER
But nineteen, at the most.

FACE Very good, Abel.

DRUGGER
Marry, she's not in fashion, yet; she wears
A hood: but 't stands a cop.

FACE No matter, Abel.

DRUGGER
And, I do, now and then give her a fucus—

FACE
What! Dost thou deal, Nab?

SUBTLE I did tell you, Captain.

25 FACE not in Q

19–24 Subtle is constructing a rebus of Drugger's name. Rebuses (which originated in France) were popular at the time. Camden mentions a man who expressed 'Rose Hill I love well' by painting the border of his gown with a rose, a hill, a loaf and a well (*Remains*, 1623, p. 145)

20 *Dee* John Dee (1527–1608); an eminent occultist patronised by Queen Elizabeth

26 *legs* bows

30 *bona roba* fine woman; prostitute

33 *a cop* on the head (a hat would have been more fashionable than a hood, but at least she wears her hood *like* a hat)

34 *fucus* a cosmetic; Face pretends to understand 'fuck'

35 *deal* do business (with sexual sense of 'get down to it')

DRUGGER
And physic too sometime, sir: for which she trusts me
With all her mind. She's come up here, of purpose
To learn the fashion.
FACE
Good (his match too!) on, Nab.
DRUGGER
And she does strangely long to know her fortune.
FACE
God's lid, Nab, send her to the Doctor, hither.
DRUGGER
Yes, I have spoke to her of his worship, already:
But she's afraid, it will be blown abroad
And hurt her marriage.
FACE
Hurt it? 'Tis the way
To heal it, if 'twere hurt; to make it more
Followed, and sought: Nab, thou shalt tell her this.
She'll be more known, more talked of, and your widows
Are ne'er of any price till they be famous;
Their honour is their multitude of suitors:
Send her, it may be thy good fortune. What?
Thou dost not know.
DRUGGER
No, sir, she'll never marry
Under a knight. Her brother has made a vow.
FACE
What, and dost thou despair, my little Nab,
Knowing, what the Doctor has set down for thee,
And, seeing so many, o' the city, dubbed?
One glass o' thy water, with a Madam, I know,
Will have it done, Nab. What's her brother? A knight?
DRUGGER
No, sir, a gentleman, newly warm in his land, sir,
Scarce cold in his one and twenty; that does govern
His sister, here: and is a man himself
Of some three thousand a year, and is come up
To learn to quarrel, and to live by his wits,
And will go down again, and die i' the country.
FACE
How! To quarrel?
DRUGGER
Yes, sir, to carry quarrels,
As gallants do, and manage 'em, by line.
FACE
'Slid, Nab! The Doctor is the only man

54 *dubbed* knighted; James I notoriously raised money by selling knighthoods to the new rich

57 *newly warm in* who has just gained

64 *by line* by rules

In Christendom for him. He has made a table,
With mathematical demonstrations,
Touching the art of quarrels. He will give him
An instrument to quarrel by. Go, bring 'em, both:
Him, and his sister. And, for thee, with her
The Doctor haply may persuade. Go to.
Shalt give his worship, a new damask suit
Upon the premises.

SUBTLE
O, good Captain.

FACE
He shall,
He is the honestest fellow, Doctor, Stay not,
No offers, bring the damask, and the parties.

DRUGGER
I'll try my power, sir.

FACE
And thy will too, Nab.

SUBTLE
'Tis good tobacco this! What is't an ounce?

FACE
He'll send you a pound, Doctor.

SUBTLE
O, no.

FACE
He will do't.
It is the goodest soul. Abel, about it.
(Thou shalt know more anon. Away, be gone.)
[*Exit* DRUGGER]
A miserable rogue, and lives with cheese,
And has the worms. That was the cause indeed
Why he came now. He dealt with me, in private,
To get a med'cine for 'em.

SUBTLE
And shall, sir. This works.

FACE
A wife, a wife, for one on's, my dear Subtle:
We'll e'en draw lots, and he, that fails, shall have
The more in goods, the other has in tail.

SUBTLE
Rather the less. For she may be so light
She may want grains.

FACE
Ay, or be such a burden,
A man would scarce endure her, for the whole.

74 *Stay not* Say not Q

---

66 *table* diagram, visual scheme
85 *on's* of us
87 *in tail* puns on 1) genital satisfaction ('tail' is still used in this sense) and 2) entail – a settlement of succession to an estate
89 *grains* a grain is the smallest unit of weight, based upon a grain of corn or wheat

SUBTLE
Faith, best let's see her first, and then determine.
FACE
Content. But Dol must ha' no breath on't.
SUBTLE
Mum.
Away, you to your Surly yonder, catch him.
FACE
Pray God, I ha' not stayed too long.
SUBTLE
I fear it.
[*Exeunt*]

Act III, Scene i

[*In the street outside Lovewit's house*]

[*Enter*] TRIBULATION, ANANIAS

TRIBULATION
These chastisements are common to the Saints,
And such rebukes we of the Separation
Must bear, with willing shoulders, as the trials
Sent forth, to tempt our frailties.
ANANIAS
In pure zeal,
I do not like the man: he is a heathen.
And speaks the language of Canaan, truly.
TRIBULATION
I think him a profane person, indeed.
ANANIAS
He bears
The visible mark of the Beast, in his forehead.
And for his stone, it is a work of darkness,
And, with philosophy, blinds the eyes of man.
TRIBULATION
Good Brother, we must bend unto all means,
That may give furtherance, to the holy cause.

2–4 *we of the . . . Sent forth* th'Elect must beare, with patience;/They are the exercises of the Spirit,/And sent Q

---

2 *Separation* the Anabaptists believed themselves to be the elect, separate from all others

6 *the language of Canaan* as opposed to Hebrew or their Puritan idiolect; 'In that day shall five cities in the land of Egypt speak the language of Canaan', *Isaiah* xix.18

8 *mark of the Beast Revelation* xvi.2, xix.20

ANANIAS
Which his cannot: the sanctified cause
Should have a sanctified course.
TRIBULATION Not always necessary.
The children of perdition are, oft-times,
Made instruments even of the greatest works.
Beside, we should give somewhat to man's nature,
The place he lives in, still about the fire,
And fume of metals, that intoxicate
The brain of man, and make him prone to passion.
Where have you greater atheists, than your cooks?
Or more profane, or choleric than your glassmen?
More antichristian, than your bell-founders?
What makes the Devil so devilish, I would ask you,
Satan, our common enemy, but his being
Perpetually about the fire, and boiling
Brimstone, and arsenic? We must give, I say,
Unto the motives, and the stirrers up
Of humours in the blood. It may be so.
When as the work is done, the stone is made,
This heat of his may turn into a zeal,
And stand up for the beauteous discipline,
Against the menstruous cloth, and rag of Rome.
We must await his calling, and the coming
Of the good spirit. You did fault, t' upbraid him
With the Brethren's blessing of Heidelberg, weighing
What need we have, to hasten on the work,
For the restoring of the silenced Saints,
Which ne'er will be, but by the philosopher's stone.
And, so a learned Elder, one of Scotland,
Assured me; *aurum potabile* being
The only med'cine, for the civil magistrate,
T' incline him to a feeling of the cause:
And must be daily used, in the disease.

15–16 *The children . . . works* this concept of evil being, in spite of itself, an agent for good was a familiar one. Shakespeare's Richard III is an example

17 *give* concede 18 *still* always

33 *rag of Rome* the Puritans identified the Church of Rome with the scarlet clad woman of *Revelation* xvii. Here the red surplice worn by Roman bishops is identified with rags stained with menstrual blood. The alchemists also used a *menstruum*; the words could be taken in three different ways (alchemical, theological, gynaecological) according to the situation of the hearer

38 *the silenced Saints* puritan clergy excommunicated for non-conformity after the Hampton Court conference of 1604; they were known as the 'silenced ministers'

41 *aurum potabile* drinkable gold; bribery is intended here

ANANIAS
I have not edified more, truly, by man;
Not, since the beautiful light, first, shone on me:
And I am sad, my zeal hath so offended.
TRIBULATION
Let us call on him, then.
ANANIAS The motion's good,
And of the spirit; I will knock first:
[*Knocks*]
Peace be within.

Act III, Scene ii

[*Inside Lovewit's house*]

[*Enter*] SUBTLE

SUBTLE
O, are you come? 'Twas time. Your threescore minutes
Were at the last thread, you see; and down had gone
Furnus acediae, turris circulatorius:
Lembic, bolt's head, retort, and pelican
Had all been cinders. Wicked Ananias!
Art thou returned? Nay then, it goes down, yet.
TRIBULATION
Sir, be appeased, he is come to humble
Himself in spirit, and to ask your patience,
If too much zeal hath carried him, aside,
From the due path.
SUBTLE Why, this doth qualify!
TRIBULATION
The Brethren had no purpose, verily,
To give you the least grievance: but are ready
To lend their willing hands, to any project
The spirit, and you direct.
SUBTLE This qualifies more!

48 *motion* intention
3 *Furnus acediae* 'the furnace of sloth'; the same as the 'lazy Henry' of II.v.80 *turris circulatorius* circulating tower; an apparatus for continuous circulation and refinement
4 *Lembic* alembic
10 *qualify* mitigate

TRIBULATION

And, for the orphans' goods, let them be valued,
Or what is needful, else, to the holy work,
It shall be numbered: here, by me, the Saints
Throw down their purse before you.

SUBTLE This qualifies, most!

Why, thus it should be, now you understand.
Have I discoursed so unto you, of our stone?
And, of the good that it shall bring your cause?
Showed you, (beside the main of hiring forces
Abroad, drawing the Hollanders, your friends,
From th' Indies, to serve you, with all their fleet)
That even the med'cinal use shall make you a faction,
And party in the realm? As, put the case,
That some great man in state, he have the gout,
Why, you but send three drops of your elixir,
You help him straight: there you have made a friend.
Another has the palsy, or the dropsy,
He takes of your incombustible stuff,
He's young again: there you have made a friend.
A lady, that is past the feat of body,
Though not of mind, and hath her face decayed
Beyond all cure of paintings, you restore
With the oil of talc; there you have made a friend:
And all her friends. A lord, that is a leper,
A knight, that has the bone-ache, or a squire
That hath both these, you make 'em smooth, and sound,
With a bare fricace of your medicine: still,
You increase your friends.

TRIBULATION Ay, 'tis very pregnant.

SUBTLE

And, then, the turning of this lawyer's pewter
To plate, at Christmas—

ANANIAS Christ-tide, I pray you.

35 *paintings* painting Q

---

17 *by me* in my person

25–6 *That even . . . realm* you'll become a force to be reckoned with in the country merely through the influence you'll gain from its medical effects

33 *feat of body* copulation

35 *paintings* cosmetics

36 *oil of talc* white elixir used by alchemists; this contrasts with the cosmetic used to whiten the skin

40 *fricace* rubbing

41 *pregnant* persuasive; full of sense

SUBTLE
Yet, Ananias?
ANANIAS I have done.
SUBTLE Or changing
His parcel gilt, to massy gold. You cannot
But raise your friends. Withal, to be of power
To pay an army, in the field, to buy
The king of France, out of his realms; or Spain,
Out of his Indies: what can you not do,
Against lords spiritual, or temporal,
That shall oppone you?
TRIBULATION Verily, 'tis true.
We may be temporal lords, ourselves, I take it.
SUBTLE
You may be anything, and leave off to make
Long-winded exercises: or suck up,
Your ha, and hum, in a tune. I not deny,
But such as are not graced, in a state,
May, for their ends, be adverse in religion,
And get a tune, to call the flock together:
For (to say sooth) a tune does much, with women,
And other phlegmatic people, it is your bell.
ANANIAS
Bells are profane: a tune may be religious.
SUBTLE
No warning with you? Then, farewell my patience.
'Slight, it shall down: I will not be thus tortured.
TRIBULATION
I pray you, sir.
SUBTLE All shall perish. I have spoke it.
TRIBULATION
Let me find grace, sir, in your eyes; the man
He stands corrected: neither did his zeal
(But as yourself) allow a tune, somewhere.
Which, now, being toward the stone, we shall not need.
SUBTLE
No, nor your holy vizard, to win widows

45 *parcel gilt* partly gilded stuff
51 *oppone* oppose
55 *I not* I do not
61 *Bells are profane* bells had popish associations
63 *it shall down* i.e. the alchemical apparatus
69–97 *No, nor... the Disciple* Subtle continues to expose the Anabaptists' craft and hypocrisy to the audience while Ananias and Tribulation remain oblivious
69 *holy vizard* pious appearance

To give you legacies; or make zealous wives
To rob their husbands, for the common cause:
Nor take the start of bonds, broke but one day,
And say, they were forfeited, by providence.
Nor shall you need, o'er-night, to eat huge meals,
To celebrate your next day's fast the better:
The whilst the Brethren, and the Sisters, humbled,
Abate the stiffness of the flesh. Nor cast
Before your hungry hearers, scrupulous bones,
As whether a Christian may hawk, or hunt;
Or whether, matrons, of the holy assembly,
May lay their hair out, or wear doublets:
Or have that idol Starch, about their linen.

ANANIAS
It is, indeed, an idol.

TRIBULATION
Mind him not, sir.
I do command thee, spirit (of zeal, but trouble)
To peace within him. Pray you, sir, go on.

SUBTLE
Nor shall you need to libel 'gainst the prelates,
And shorten so your ears, against the hearing
Of the next wire-drawn grace. Nor, of necessity,
Rail against plays, to please the alderman,
Whose daily custard you devour. Nor lie
With zealous rage, till you are hoarse. Not one
Of these so singular arts. Nor call yourselves,
By names of Tribulation, Persecution,

72 *take the start* take advantage of

77 *Abate the stiffness of the flesh* we (but not Ananias and Tribulation) should hear the sexual innuendo here

78 *scrupulous bones* trivial bones of contention

79 *hawk ... hunt* 'I neuer read of any, in *the* volume of *the* sacred scripture, that was a good man and a Hunter'; Stubbes, *The Anatomie of the Abuses in England in Shakespeare's Youth*, ed. Furnivall, 1877–9, part i, p. 181

81 *lay their hair out, or wear doublets* 'Then followeth the trimming and tricking of their heds in laying out their hair to the shewe, which of force must be curled, frisled and crisped, laid out (a World to see!) on wreathes & borders from one eare to an other' (ibid. p. 67) and (re. *Deuteronomy* xxii 5) 'The Women also there haue dublets & Ierkins, as men haue heer ... & though this be a kinde of attire appropriate onely to man, yet they blush not to wear it' (ibid. p. 73)

82 *that idol Starch* 'The deuils liquore, I mean *Starch*' (ibid. p. 70)

84–5 *I do ... him* Tribulation is attempting to placate the troubled spirit that possesses Ananias

87 *shorten so your ears* have your ears cut off or clipped as a punishment

88 *wire-drawn grace* extended prayer (grace) before eating

90 *custard* a kind of open pie; a bit like *quiche*

Restraint, Long-Patience, and such like, affected
By the whole family, or wood of you,
Only for glory, and to catch the ear
Of the disciple.

TRIBULATION Truly, sir, they are
Ways, that the godly Brethren have invented,
For propagation of the glorious cause,
As very notable means, and whereby, also,
Themselves grow soon, and profitably famous.

SUBTLE
O, but the stone, all's idle to it! Nothing!
The art of angels, nature's miracle,
The divine secret, that doth fly in clouds,
From east to west: and whose tradition
Is not from men, but spirits.

ANANIAS I hate traditions:
I do not trust 'em—

TRIBULATION Peace.

ANANIAS They are Popish, all.
I will not peace. I will not—

TRIBULATION Ananias.

ANANIAS
Please the profane, to grieve the godly: I may not.

SUBTLE
Well, Ananias, thou shalt overcome.

TRIBULATION
It is an ignorant zeal, that haunts him, sir.
But truly, else, a very faithful Brother,
A botcher: and a man, by revelation,
That hath a competent knowledge of the truth.

SUBTLE
Has he a competent sum, there, i' the bag,
To buy the goods, within? I am made guardian,
And must, for charity, and conscience' sake,

99 *glorious* holy Q

---

95 *wood* a gathering of family trees; 'wood' also meant 'mad' – a good collective noun for extremists

106 *I hate traditions* some Puritans recognised only the authority of the Bible and direct revelation. Traditions were associated with the Church of Rome and Judaism

113 *botcher* probably used in the specialised sense of 'tailor'; John of Leyden, the Anabaptist 'King', had been a tailor and is called 'the botcher' by Thomas Nashe in his description of the occupation of Münster in *The Unfortunate Traveller*, ed. J. B. Steane, Harmondsworth, 1972, p. 277

Now, see the most be made, for my poor orphan:
Though I desire the Brethren, too, good gainers.
There, they are, within. When you have viewed, and
bought 'em,
And ta'en the inventory of what they are,
They are ready for projection; there's no more
To do: cast on the med'cine, so much silver
As there is tin there, so much gold as brass,
I'll gi' it you in, by weight.

TRIBULATION But how long time,
Sir, must the Saints expect, yet?

SUBTLE Let me see,
How's the moon, now? Eight, nine, ten days hence
He will be silver potate; then, three days,
Before he citronize: some fifteen days,
The *magisterium* will be perfected.

ANANIAS
About the second day, of the third week,
In the ninth month?

SUBTLE Yes, my good Ananias.

TRIBULATION
What will the orphans' goods arise to, think you?

SUBTLE
Some hundred marks; as much as filled three cars,
Unladed now: you'll make six millions of 'em
But I must ha' more coals laid in.

TRIBULATION How!

SUBTLE Another load,
And then we ha' finished. We must now increase
Our fire to *ignis ardens*, we are past
Fimus equinus, balnei, cineris,
And all those lenter heats. If the holy purse
Should, with this draught, fall low, and that the Saints
Do need a present sum, I have a trick

135 *you'll* you shall Q
142 *have a trick* F2 have trick Q, F

---

128 *silver potate* liquid silver
129 *citronize* turn yellow – a sign that the work is near completion
134 *cars* carts
138 *ignis ardens* the hottest fire
139 *Fimus equinus* the lowest form of heat, produced by horse dung
balnei see II.iii.41
cineris the heat of ashes
140 *lenter* slower

To melt the pewter, you shall buy now, instantly,
And, with a tincture, make you as good Dutch dollars,
As any are in Holland.

TRIBULATION Can you so?

SUBTLE
Ay, and shall bide the third examination.

ANANIAS
It will be joyful tidings to the Brethren.

SUBTLE
But you must carry it, secret.

TRIBULATION Ay, but stay,
This act of coining, is it lawful?

ANANIAS Lawful?
We know no magistrate. Or, if we did,
This 's foreign coin.

SUBTLE It is no coining, sir.
It is but casting.

TRIBULATION Ha? You distinguish well.
Casting of money may be lawful.

ANANIAS 'Tis, sir.

TRIBULATION
Truly, I take it so.

SUBTLE There is no scruple,
Sir, to be made of it; believe Ananias:
This case of conscience he is studied in.

TRIBULATION
I'll make a question of it, to the Brethren.

ANANIAS
The Brethren shall approve it lawful, doubt not.
Where shall't be done.

Knock without

SUBTLE For that we'll talk, anon.
There's some to speak with me. Go in, I pray you,
And view the parcels. That's the inventory.
I'll come to you straight.

[*Exeunt* ANANIAS, TRIBULATION]

Who is it? Face! Appear.

150 *We know no magistrate* some Puritans would only accept Scriptural authority in civil matters

151–2 *It is . . . casting* the casting of foreign coin *was* as much an offence as coining English counterfeits (1 & 2 Philip and Mary, cxi)

Act III, Scene iii

[*Enter*] FACE [*dressed as Captain, to* SUBTLE]

SUBTLE
How now? Good prize?
FACE
Good pox! Yond' costive cheater
Never came on.
SUBTLE
How then?
FACE
I ha' walked the round,
Till now, and no such thing.
SUBTLE
And ha' you quit him?
FACE
Quit him? And hell would quit him too, he were happy.
'Slight, would you have me stalk like a mill-jade,
All day, for one, that will not yield us grains?
I know him of old.
SUBTLE
O, but to ha' gulled him,
Had been a mastery.
FACE
Let him go, black boy,
And turn thee, that some fresh news may possess thee.
A noble Count, a Don of Spain (my dear
Delicious compeer, and my party-bawd)
Who is come hither, private, for his conscience,
And brought munition with him, six great slops,
Bigger than three Dutch hoys, beside round trunks,
Furnished with pistolets, and pieces of eight,
Will straight be here, my rogue, to have thy bath
(That is the colour,) and to make his battery

2 *walked the round* gone round the nave (of the Temple Church – also known as 'the round')
5 *mill-jade* a horse that works a mill by moving in circles
8 *black boy* Subtle's face is darkened by the smoke of his business
9 *turn thee* shift your attention
11 *compeer* companion; mate
party-bawd part bawd, or 'bawd of my party'
13 *slops* wide breeches
14 *hoys* small sea vessels carrying passengers and goods around coastal waters
trunks trunk hose; knee breeches
15 *pistolets* Spanish gold coins
pieces of eight Spanish dollars

Upon our Dol, our castle, our Cinque-Port,
Our Dover pier, our what thou wilt. Where is she?
She must prepare perfumes, delicate linen,
The bath in chief, a banquet, and her wit,
For she must milk his epididimis.
Where is the doxy?

SUBTLE
I'll send her to thee:
And but dispatch my brace of little John Leydens,
And come again myself.

FACE
Are they within then?

SUBTLE
Numbering the sum.

FACE
How much?

SUBTLE
A hundred marks, boy.
[*Exit* SUBTLE]

FACE
Why, this 's a lucky day! Ten pounds of Mammon!
Three o' my clerk! A portague o' my grocer!
This o' the Brethren! Beside reversions,
And states, to come i' the widow, and my Count!
[*Enter* DOL]
My share, today, will not be bought for forty—

DOL
What?

FACE
Pounds, dainty Dorothy, art thou so near?

DOL
Yes, say lord General, how fares our camp?

FACE
As, with the few, that had entrenched themselves
Safe, by their discipline, against a world, Dol:
And laughed, within those trenches, and grew fat
With thinking on the booties, Dol, brought in

22 *milk* feele Q

18–19 *Cinque-Port . . . Dover pier* one of the five ports on the South-East coast of England occupying vital defence positions. Dover is the chief. Dol is a Cinque-Port because she is constantly invaded. The portals of her body and five senses may also be implied. 'Cinque' would have been pronounced 'sink'

22 *epididimis* 'A long narrow structure attached to the posterior border of the adjoining outer surface of the testicle' (*OED*); so 'milk his epididimis' = 'drain his balls'

24 *John Leydens* John Leyden led the Anabaptist occupation of Münster in 1532–6

29 *reversions* goods due in the future

33 *say . . . camp* the first line of Kyd's *The Spanish Tragedy* – a hugely popular play to which Jonson had written additions

Daily, by their small parties. This dear hour,
A doughty Don is taken, with my Dol;
And thou may'st make his ransom, what thou wilt,
My Dousabell: he shall be brought here, fettered
With thy fair looks, before he sees thee; and thrown
In a down-bed, as dark as any dungeon;
Where thou shalt keep him waking, with thy drum;
Thy drum, my Dol; thy drum; till he be tame
As the poor blackbirds were i' the great frost,
Or bees are with a basin: and so hive him
I' the swanskin coverlid, and cambric sheets,
Till he work honey, and wax, my little God's-gift.

DOL
What is he, General?

FACE An *Adalantado*,
A grandee, girl. Was not my Dapper here, yet?

DOL
No.

FACE Nor my Drugger?

DOL Neither.

FACE A pox on 'em,
They are so long a-furnishing! Such stinkards
Would not be seen, upon these festival days.
[*Enter* SUBTLE]
How now! Ha' you done?

SUBTLE Done. They are gone. The sum
Is here in bank, my Face. I would, we knew
Another chapman, now, would buy 'em outright.

FACE
'Slid, Nab shall do't, against he ha' the widow,
To furnish household.

SUBTLE Excellent, well thought on,
Pray God, he come.

FACE I pray, he keep away
Till our new business be o'erpast.

42 *Dousabell* (French) 'douce et belle': sweet and lovely
44 *drum* belly; perhaps also suggesting the beat of sexual intercourse
46 *the great frost* of 1607–8 when the Thames froze over; the blackbirds would have depended on humans for food
47 *bees . . . basin* according to Virgil (et. al.) swarming bees can be attracted by banging a metal basin (*Georgics* 4.64)
49 *wax* both noun (what Mammon will produce) and verb – 'to grow [erect]'
God's gift Dorothea means 'God's gift' in Greek
53 *a-furnishing* preparing; stocking up
57 *chapman* merchant

SUBTLE But, Face,
How camest thou, by this secret Don?
FACE A spirit
Brought me th' intelligence, in a paper, here,
As I was conjuring, yonder, in my circle
For Surly: I ha' my flies abroad. Your bath
Is famous, Subtle, by my means. Sweet Dol,
You must go tune your virginal, no losing
O' the least time. And, do you hear? Good action.
Firk, like a flounder; kiss, like a scallop, close:
And tickle him with thy mother-tongue. His great
Verdugoship has not a jot of language:
So much the easier to be cozened, my Dolly.
He will come here, in a hired coach, obscure,
And our own coachman, whom I have sent, as guide,
No creature else.

One knocks

Who's that?
SUBTLE It i' not he?
FACE
O no, not yet this hour.
SUBTLE Who is't?
DOL [*At window*] Dapper,
Your clerk.
FACE God's will, then, Queen of Fairy,
On with your tire; and, Doctor, with your robes.
Let's despatch him, for God's sake.
SUBTLE 'Twill be long.
FACE
I warrant you, take but the cues I give you,

62 FACE F2; not in Q, F
79 *Let's* Lett's vs Q

---

69 *Firk, like a flounder* the arching contortions of a flat fish out of water are suggested
kiss, like a scallop, close editors refer to a Latin poem by the Emperor Gallienus with the phrase 'non vincant oscula conchae' ('Don't let a clam's kisses win'). But Jonson wouldn't have needed this to remind him of the resemblance between shellfish and female genitals which has led many to find shellfish aphrodisiac
70 *mother-tongue* i.e. what lies between the vaginal *labia*
71 *Verdugoship verdugo* is Spanish for 'hangman'
language English
73 *obscure* concealed

It shall be brief enough. 'Slight, here are more!
Abel, and I think, the angry boy, the heir,
That fain would quarrel.

SUBTLE
And the widow?

FACE
No,
Not that I see. Away.
[*Exit* SUBTLE. FACE *opens door*]
O sir, you are welcome.

Act III, Scene iv

[*Enter*] DAPPER [*to them*]

FACE
The Doctor is within, a-moving for you;
(I have had the most ado to win him to it)
He swears, you'll be the darling o' the dice:
He never heard her Highness dote, till now (he says.)
Your aunt has given you the most gracious words,
That can be thought on.

DAPPER
Shall I see her Grace?

FACE
See her, and kiss her, too.
[*Enter* DRUGGER *and* KASTRIL]
What? Honest Nab!
Hast brought the damask?

DRUGGER
No, sir, here's tobacco.

FACE
'Tis well done, Nab: thou'lt bring the damask too?

DRUGGER
Yes, here's the gentleman, Captain, Master Kastril,
I have brought to see the Doctor.

FACE
Where's the widow?

DRUGGER
Sir, as he likes, his sister (he says) shall come.

FACE
O, is it so? 'Good time. Is your name Kastril, sir?

KASTRIL
Ay, and the best o' the Kastrils, I'd be sorry else,

4 *(he says.)* not in Q
8 DRUGGER *Nab* Q, F
9 *Nab* not in Q

82 *angry boy* 'angry boys', 'terrible boys' or, most commonly, 'roaring boys' were names given to well-heeled thugs

By fifteen hundred, a year. Where is this Doctor?
My mad tobacco-boy, here, tells me of one,
That can do things. Has he any skill?

FACE
Wherein, sir?

KASTRIL
To carry a business, manage a quarrel, fairly,
Upon fit terms.

FACE
It seems sir, you're but young
About the town, that can make that a question!

KASTRIL
Sir, not so young, but I have heard some speech
Of the angry boys, and seen 'em take tobacco;
And in his shop: and I can take it too.
And I would fain be one of 'em, and go down
And practise i' the country.

FACE
Sir, for the *duello*,
The Doctor, I assure you, shall inform you,
To the least shadow of a hair: and show you,
An instrument he has, of his own making,
Wherewith, no sooner shall you make report
Of any quarrel, but he will take the height on't,
Most instantly; and tell in what degree,
Of safety it lies in, or mortality.
And, how it may be borne, whether in a right line,
Or a half-circle; or may, else, be cast
Into an angle blunt, if not acute:
All this he will demonstrate. And then, rules,
To give, and take the lie, by.

KASTRIL
How? To take it?

FACE
Yes, in oblique, he'll show you; or in circle:
But never in diameter. The whole town
Study his theorems, and dispute them, ordinarily,
At the eating academies.

KASTRIL
But, does he teach
Living, by the wits, too?

FACE
Anything, whatever.

18–19 *manage ... terms* quarrelling, like much else, had been systematised and made into a science at this period. In *As You Like It* Touchstone goes through the degrees of the lie (V.iv.90ff)

25 *duello* duel 32 *mortality* danger

39 *in diameter* i.e. head-on; 'the lie direct'

40–1 *ordinarily ... academies* Jonson puns on the sense of 'ordinary' as eating house and reverses the expected epithets (study and disputation usually take place in academies, eating in ordinaries)

You cannot think that subtlety, but he reads it.
He made me a Captain. I was a stark pimp,
Just o' your standing, 'fore I met with him:
It i' not two months since. I'll tell you his method.
First, he will enter you, at some ordinary.

KASTRIL
No, I'll not come there. You shall pardon me.

FACE
For why, sir?

KASTRIL
There's gaming there, and tricks.

FACE
Why, would you be
A gallant, and not game?

KASTRIL
Ay, 'twill spend a man.

FACE
Spend you? It will repair you, when you are spent.
How do they live by their wits, there, that have vented
Six times your fortunes?

KASTRIL
What, three thousand a year!

FACE
Ay, forty thousand.

KASTRIL
Are there such?

FACE
Ay, sir.
And gallants, yet. Here's a young gentleman,
Is born to nothing, forty marks a year,
Which I count nothing. He's to be initiated,
And have a fly o' the Doctor. He will win you
By unresistable luck, within this fortnight,
Enough to buy a barony. They will set him
Upmost, at the Groom-porter's, all the Christmas!
And, for the whole year through, at every place,
Where there is play, present him with the chair;
The best attendance, the best drink, sometimes
Two glasses of canary, and pay nothing;
The purest linen, and the sharpest knife,
The partridge next his trencher: and, somewhere,
The dainty bed, in private, with the dainty.
You shall ha' your ordinaries bid for him,
As playhouses for a poet; and the master

43 *reads* understands
44 *stark* arrant, unmodified
50 *spend a man* waste away a man's wealth
58 *fly* see Argument, l.11
61 *Groom-porter* an officer in the royal household particularly concerned with gaming regulations
64 *attendance* service 65 *canary* canary wine

Pray him, aloud, to name what dish he affects,
Which must be buttered shrimps: and those that drink
To no mouth else, will drink to his, as being
The goodly, president mouth of all the board.

KASTRIL
Do you not gull one?

FACE
'Od's my life! Do you think it?
You shall have a cast commander, (can but get
In credit with a glover, or a spurrier,
For some two pair, of either's ware, aforehand)
Will, by most swift posts, dealing with him,
Arrive at competent means, to keep himself,
His punk, and naked boy, in excellent fashion.
And be admired for it.

KASTRIL
Will the Doctor teach this?

FACE
He will do more, sir, when your land is gone,
(As men of spirit hate to keep earth long)
In a vacation, when small money is stirring,
And ordinaries suspended till the term,
He'll show a perspective, where on one side
You shall behold the faces, and the persons
Of all sufficient young heirs, in town,
Whose bonds are current for commodity;
On th' other side, the merchants' forms, and others,
That, without help of any second broker,
(Who would expect a share) will trust such parcels:
In the third square, the very street, and sign
Where the commodity dwells, and does but wait
To be delivered, be it pepper, soap,
Hops, or tobacco, oatmeal, woad, or cheeses.
All which you may so handle, to enjoy,
To your own use, and never stand obliged.

75 *'Od's my life* God's my life Q

---

71 *affects* desires
76 *cast commander* unemployed officer
77 *spurrier* spur-maker
79 *by most swift posts* with great speed
81 *punk* prostitute, kept woman
naked boy just that; 'catamite' is the grander term
84 *As men . . . long* this has the logic of a natural law: earth descends, spirit rises
87 *perspective* optical trick
90 *commodity* see II.i.10–14
97 *woad* a blue dye

KASTRIL
I' faith! Is he such a fellow?
FACE
Why, Nab here knows him.
And then for making matches, for rich widows,
Young gentlewomen, heirs, the fortunat'st man!
He's sent to, far, and near, all over England,
To have his counsel, and to know their fortunes.
KASTRIL
God's will, my suster shall see him.
FACE
I'll tell you, sir,
What he did tell me of Nab. It's a strange thing!
(By the way you must eat no cheese, Nab, it breeds melancholy:
And that same melancholy breeds worms) but pass it –
He told me, honest Nab, here, was ne'er at tavern,
But once in's life.
DRUGGER
Truth, and no more I was not.
FACE
And, then he was so sick—
DRUGGER
Could he tell you that, too?
FACE
How should I know it?
DRUGGER
In troth we had been a-shooting,
And had a piece of fat ram-mutton, to supper,
That lay so heavy o' my stomach—
FACE
And he has no head
To bear any wine; for, what with the noise o' the fiddlers,
And care of his shop, for he dares keep no servants—
DRUGGER
My head did so ache—
FACE
As he was fain to be brought home,
The Doctor told me. And then, a good old woman—
DRUGGER
(Yes, faith, she dwells in Sea-coal Lane) did cure me,

107 *eat . . . melancholy* milk and its products were thought to engender melancholy. In fact they stimulate the production of mucus and, if anything, promote a phlegmatic disposition

109–26 *He told . . . the Doctor* Face's prompting shows him to know Dapper's story – and its wording – by heart

119 *Sea-coal Lane* now Old Seacoal Lane, running from Farringdon Street to Fleet Lane. It was the home of fruiterers

With sodden ale, and pellitory o' the wall:
Cost me but two pence. I had another sickness,
Was worse than that.

FACE Ay, that was with the grief
Thou took'st for being 'sessed at eighteen pence,
For the water-work.

DRUGGER In truth, and it was like
T'have cost me almost my life.

FACE Thy hair went off?

DRUGGER
Yes, sir, 'twas done for spite.

FACE Nay, so says the Doctor.

KASTRIL
Pray thee, tobacco-boy, go fetch my suster,
I'll see this learned boy, before I go:
And so shall she.

FACE Sir, he is busy now:
But, if you have a sister to fetch hither,
Perhaps, your own pains may command her sooner;
And he, by that time, will be free.

KASTRIL I go. [*Exit* KASTRIL]

FACE
Drugger, she's thine: the damask. [*Exit* DRUGGER]
(Subtle, and I
Must wrestle for her.) Come on, master Dapper.
You see, how I turn clients, here, away,
To give your cause dispatch. Ha' you performed
The ceremonies were enjoined you?

DAPPER Yes, o' the vinegar,
And the clean shirt.

FACE 'Tis well: that shirt may do you
More worship than you think. Your aunt's afire,
But that she will not show it, t'have a sight on you.
Ha' you provided for her Grace's servants?

DAPPER
Yes, here are six score Edward shillings.

FACE Good.

132 *go* go, Sir Q

---

120 *sodden* boiled
pellitory o' the wall lichwort (of the same family as stinging nettle and hop); this bushy plant which grows in the cracks of walls is used in decoctions and infusions as a remedy for urinary disorders

123 *'sessed* assessed (for a rate)

124 *the water-work* see II.i.76. The 'New River', an aqueduct, was under construction at the time the play was written

126 *'twas done for spite* i.e. the excessive levy

DAPPER
And an old Harry's sovereign.
FACE
Very good.
DAPPER
And three James shillings, and an Elizabeth groat,
Just twenty nobles.
FACE
O, you are too just.
I would you had had the other noble in Marys.
DAPPER
I have some Philip, and Marys.
FACE
Ay, those same
Are best of all. Where are they? Hark, the Doctor.

Act III, Scene v

[*Enter*] SUBTLE *disguised like a Priest of Fairy* [*to them*]

SUBTLE
Is yet her Grace's cousin come?
FACE
He is come.
SUBTLE
And is he fasting?
FACE
Yes.
SUBTLE
And hath cried *hum*?
FACE
Thrice, you must answer.
DAPPER
Thrice.
SUBTLE
And as oft *buz*?
FACE
If you have, say.

143 *old Harry's sovereign* a sovereign from the realm of either Henry VII or Henry VIII; worth only 10 shillings
144 *James shillings* i.e. shillings from the present realm
groat fourpence
145 *nobles* worth 6 shillings and 8 pence
147 *Philip and Marys* these nobles had the heads of the two sovereigns facing each other. Face, true to his name, seems to want his coins to provide a portrait gallery. There was a slight, but insignificant reduction in the fineness of gold coins between the reigns of Mary and James, so Face's enthusiasm for the earlier coins is not based on greed for gold
III.v *H.&S.* cite Edward Marchant's *The seuerall Notorious and lewd Cosenages of Iohn West, and Alice West, falsely called the King and Queen of Fayries*. These two were convicted in 1613 of practices very similar to those described in this scene. Jonson may well have heard of them

DAPPER
I have.

SUBTLE
Then, to her coz,
Hoping, that he hath vinegared his senses,
As he was bid, the Fairy Queen dispenses,
By me, this robe, the petticoat of Fortune;
Which that he straight put on, she doth importune.
And though to Fortune near be her petticoat,
Yet, nearer is her smock, the Queen doth note:
And, therefore, even of that a piece she hath sent,
Which, being a child, to wrap him in, was rent;
And prays him, for a scarf, he now will wear it

They blind him with a rag

(With as much love, as then her Grace did tear it)
About his eyes, to show, he is fortunate.
And, trusting unto her to make his state,
He'll throw away all worldly pelf, about him;
Which that he will perform, she doth not doubt him.

FACE
She need not doubt him, sir. Alas, he has nothing,
But what he will part withall, as willingly,
Upon her Grace's word (throw away your purse)

He throws away, as they bid him

As she would ask it: (handkerchiefs, and all)
She cannot bid that thing, but he'll obey.
(If you have a ring, about you, cast it off,
Or a silver seal, at your wrist, her Grace will send
Her fairies here to search you, therefore deal
Directly with her Highness. If they find
That you conceal a mite, you are undone.)

DAPPER
Truly, there's all.

FACE
All what?

DAPPER
My money, truly.

FACE
Keep nothing, that is transitory, about you.
(Bid Dol play music.) Look, the elves are come

DOL *enters with a cithern: they pinch him*

To pinch you, if you tell not truth. Advise you.

DAPPER
O, I have a paper with a spur-rial in't.

17 *pelf* property; stuff
32 *cithern* ghittern; an instrument like a guitar
33 *spur-rial* Edward IV noble with a blazing sun on the tail side, resembling the rowel of a spur

FACE *Ti, ti,*
They knew't, they say.
SUBTLE *Ti, ti, ti, ti,* he has more yet.
FACE
Ti, ti-ti-ti. I' the tother pocket?
SUBTLE *Titi, titi, titi, titi.*
They must pinch him, or he will never confess, they say.
DAPPER
O, O.
FACE Nay, 'pray you hold. He is her Grace's nephew.
Ti, ti, ti, ? What care you? Good faith, you shall care.
Deal plainly, sir, and shame the fairies. Show
You are an innocent.
DAPPER By this good light, I ha' nothing.
SUBTLE
Ti, ti, titi to ta. He does equivocate, she says:
Ti, ti do ti, ti ti do, ti da. And swears by the light, when he is blinded.
DAPPER
By this good dark, I ha' nothing but a half crown
Of gold, about my wrist, that my love gave me;
And a leaden heart I wore, sin' she forsook me.
FACE
I thought, 'twas something. And, would you incur
Your aunt's displeasure for these trifles? Come,
I had rather you had thrown away twenty half crowns.
You may wear your leaden heart still. [DOL *at window*]
How now?
SUBTLE
What news, Dol?
DOL Yonder's your knight, sir Mammon.
FACE
God's lid, we never thought of him, till now.
Where is he?
DOL Here, hard by. He's at the door.
SUBTLE
[*To* FACE] And, you are not ready, now? Dol, get his suit.
He must not be sent back. [*Exit* DOL]
FACE O, by no means.
What shall we do with this same puffin, here,
Now he's o' the spit?

41 *equivocate* evade
45 *leaden heart* an emblem of grief
56 *o' the spit* ready for roasting

SUBTLE
Why, lay him back a while,
With some device.

[*Enter* DOL]

Ti, ti ti, ti ti ti. Would her Grace speak with me?
I come. Help, Dol.

He speaks through the keyhole, the other knocking

FACE
Who's there? Sir Epicure;
My master's i' the way. Please you to walk
Three or four turns, but till his back be turned,
And I am for you. Quickly, Dol.

[FACE *dresses as 'Lungs'*]

SUBTLE
Her Grace
Commends her kindly to you, master Dapper.

DAPPER
I long to see her Grace.

SUBTLE
She, now, is set
At dinner, in her bed; and she has sent you,
From her own private trencher, a dead mouse,
And a piece of gingerbread, to be merry withal,
And stay your stomach, lest you faint with fasting:
Yet, if you could hold out, till she saw you (she says)
It would be better for you.

FACE
Sir, he shall
Hold out, and 'twere this two hours, for her Highness;
I can assure you that. We will not lose
All we ha' done—

SUBTLE
He must nor see, nor speak
To anybody, till then.

FACE
For that, we'll put, sir,
A stay in 's mouth.

SUBTLE
Of what?

FACE
Of gingerbread.
Make you it fit. He that hath pleased her Grace,
Thus far, shall not now crinkle, for a little.
Gape sir, and let him fit you. [SUBTLE *inserts gag*]

SUBTLE
Where shall we now
Bestow him?

DOL
I' the privy.

SUBTLE
Come along, sir,
I now must show you Fortune's privy lodgings.

74 *stay* gag 76 *crinkle* shrink from his purpose

77 *let him fit you* the term to 'fit' someone could have sinister undertones; e.g. *The Spanish Tragedy*, IV.i.70, 'Why then I'll fit you'

78 *privy* private place; i.e. lavatory

FACE
Are they perfumed? And his bath ready?
SUBTLE
All.
Only the fumigation's somewhat strong.
FACE
Sir Epicure, I am yours, sir, by and by.
[*Exeunt* SUBTLE, DOL, DAPPER]

Act IV, Scene i

[*Enter*] MAMMON [*to* FACE]

FACE
O, sir, you're come i' the only, finest time—
MAMMON
Where's master?
FACE
Now preparing for projection, sir.
Your stuff will b' all changed shortly.
MAMMON
Into gold?
FACE
To gold, and silver, sir.
MAMMON
Silver, I care not for.
FACE
Yes, sir, a little to give beggars.
MAMMON
Where's the lady?
FACE
At hand, here. I ha' told her such brave things, o' you,
Touching your bounty and your noble spirit—
MAMMON
Hast thou?
FACE
As she is almost in her fit to see you.
But, good sir, no divinity i' your conference,
For fear of putting her in rage—
MAMMON
I warrant thee.
FACE
Six men will not hold her down. And then,
If the old man should hear, or see you—
MAMMON
Fear not.
FACE
The very house, sir, would run mad. You know it
How scrupulous he is, and violent,
'Gainst the least act of sin. Physic, or mathematics,

6 *o' you* on you Q

---

9 *divinity* theology

Poetry, state, or bawdry (as I told you)
She will endure, and never startle: but
No word of controversy.

MAMMON I am schooled, good Ulen.

FACE
And you must praise her house, remember that,
And her nobility.

MAMMON Let me, alone:
No herald, no nor antiquary, Lungs,
Shall do it better. Go.

FACE (Why, this is yet
A kind of modern happiness, to have
Dol Common for a great lady.) [*Exit* FACE]

MAMMON Now, Epicure,
Heighten thyself, talk to her, all in gold;
Rain her as many showers, as Jove did drops
Unto his Danae: show the God a miser,
Compared with Mammon. What? The stone will do't.
She shall feel gold, taste gold, hear gold, sleep gold:
Nay, we will *concumbere* gold. I will be puissant,
And mighty in my talk to her! Here she comes.

[*Enter* FACE, DOL]

FACE
To him, Dol, suckle him. This is the noble knight,
I told your ladyship—

MAMMON Madam, with your pardon,
I kiss your vesture.

DOL Sir, I were uncivil
If I would suffer that, my lip to you, sir.

MAMMON
I hope, my lord your brother be in health, lady?

DOL
My lord, my brother is, though I no lady, sir.

FACE
(Well said my Guinea bird.)

MAMMON Right noble madam—

18 *Ulen* Lungs Q

---

16 *state* matters of state; politics
17 *startle* be startled
23 *modern* commonplace (and so a play on Dol's name); the sense 'contemporary' was also present
26–7 *Rain . . . Danae* see II.i.102
30 *concumbere* lit. 'lie together' which Mammon seems to use as a transitive verb 'to generate'
puissant (Fr.) powerful; Mammon perhaps means 'potent'
38 *Guinea bird* guinea hen and guinea bird were slang terms for prostitute

FACE
(O, we shall have most fierce idolatry!)
MAMMON
'Tis your prerogative.
DOL
Rather your courtesy.
MAMMON
Were there nought else t'enlarge your virtues, to me,
These answers speak your breeding, and your blood.
DOL
Blood we boast none, sir, a poor baron's daughter.
MAMMON
Poor! And gat you? Profane not. Had your father
Slept all the happy remnant of his life
After the act, lain but there still, and panted,
He'd done enough, to make himself, his issue,
And his posterity noble.
DOL
Sir, although
We may be said to want the gilt, and trappings,
The dress of honour; yet we strive to keep
The seeds, and the materials.
MAMMON
I do see
The old ingredient, virtue, was not lost,
Nor the drug money, used to make your compound.
There is a strange nobility, i' your eye,
This lip, that chin! Methinks you do resemble
One o' the Austriac princes.
FACE
(Very like,
Her father was an Irish costermonger.)
MAMMON
The house of Valois, just, had such a nose.
And such a forehead, yet, the Medici
Of Florence boast.
DOL
Troth, and I have been likened
To all these princes.
FACE
(I'll be sworn, I heard it.)
MAMMON
I know not how. It is not any one,
But e'en the very choice of all their features.
FACE
(I'll in, and laugh.) [*Exit* FACE]

51–3 *The seeds . . . compound* Dol and Mammon converse in alchemical metaphors
57 *Irish costermonger* at that time many of the London street vendors were Irish
58–9 *Valois . . . Medici* great European houses but not physiognomically marked. Mammon is name-dropping

MAMMON A certain touch, or air,
That sparkles a divinity, beyond
An earthly beauty!
DOL O, you play the courtier.
MAMMON
Good lady, gi' me leave—
DOL In faith, I may not,
To mock me, sir.
MAMMON To burn i' this sweet flame:
The Phoenix never knew a nobler death.
DOL
Nay, now you court the courtier: and destroy
What you would build. This art, sir, i' your words,
Calls your whole faith in question.
MAMMON By my soul—
DOL
Nay, oaths are made o' the same air, sir.
MAMMON Nature
Never bestowed upon mortality,
A more unblamed, a more harmonious feature:
She played the stepdame in all faces, else.
Sweet madam, le' me be particular—
DOL
Particular, sir? I pray you, know your distance.
MAMMON
In no ill sense, sweet lady, but to ask
How your fair graces pass the hours? I see
You're lodged, here, i' the house of a rare man,
An excellent artist: but, what's that to you?
DOL
Yes, sir. I study here the mathematics,
And distillation.
MAMMON O, I cry your pardon.
He's a divine instructor! Can extract
The souls of all things, by his art; call all
The virtues, and the miracles of the sun,
Into a temperate furnace: teach dull nature
What her own forces are. A man, the Emperor
Has courted, above Kelley: sent his medals,

69 *Phoenix* a unique and legendary bird that builds its own funeral pyre at regular intervals and, from its own ashes, is born again

70 *court the courtier* use elaborate courtly language

78 *particular* Mammon *could* mean 'let me go into more detail'; but Dol takes 'particular' to mean 'familiar', 'intimate'

90 *Kelley* Edward Kelley (1555–95) who worked with John Dee as his 'scryer'

And chains, t' invite him.

DOL
Ay, and for his physic, sir—

MAMMON
Above the art of Æsculapius,
That drew the envy of the Thunderer!
I know all this, and more.

DOL
Troth, I am taken, sir,
Whole, with these studies, that contemplate nature.

MAMMON
It is a noble humour. But, this form
Was not intended to so dark a use!
Had you been crooked, foul, of some coarse mould,
A cloister had done well: but, such a feature
That might stand up the glory of a kingdom,
To live recluse!—is a mere solecism,
Though in a nunnery. It must not be.
I muse, my lord your brother will permit it!
You should spend half my land first, were I he.
Does not this diamant better, on my finger,
Than i' the quarry?

DOL
Yes.

MAMMON
Why, you are like it.
You were created, lady, for the light!
Here, you shall wear it; take it, the first pledge
Of what I speak: to bind you, to believe me.

DOL
In chains of adamant?

MAMMON
Yes, the strongest bands.
And take a secret, too. Here, by your side,
Doth stand, this hour, the happiest man, in Europe.

107 *the light* light Q
112 *in* of Q

---

91 *chains* these recall the fact that the Emperor Rudolph of Germany imprisoned Kelley for failing to produce the Philosopher's Stone

92 *Æsculapius* son of Apollo and god of medicine. He was able to restore men to life until Jupiter ('the Thunderer') killed him with a thunderbolt in order that men should not be immortal

96–7; 105–8 compare this specious argument with that used by Milton's Comus to the Lady (*Comus*, ll.709–754)

101 *recluse* as a recluse
solecism error

105 *diamant* diamond

110 *adamant* puns on 'a diamant'

DOL
You are contented, sir?
MAMMON Nay, in true being:
The envy of princes, and the fear of states.
DOL
Say you so, Sir Epicure!
MAMMON Yes, and thou shalt prove it,
Daughter of honour. I have cast mine eye
Upon thy form, and I will rear this beauty,
Above all styles.
DOL You mean no treason, sir!
MAMMON
No, I will take away that jealousy.
I am the lord of the philosopher's stone,
And thou the lady.
DOL How sir! Ha' you that?
MAMMON
I am the master of the mastery.
This day, the good old wretch, here, o' the house
Has made it for us. Now, he's at projection.
Think therefore, thy first wish, now; let me hear it:
And it shall rain into thy lap, no shower,
But floods of gold, whole cataracts, a deluge,
To get a nation on thee!
DOL You are pleased, sir,
To work on the ambition of our sex.
MAMMON
I am pleased, the glory of her sex should know,
This nook, here, of the Friars, is no climate
For her, to live obscurely in, to learn
Physic, and surgery, for the Constable's wife
Of some odd Hundred in Essex; but come forth,
And taste the air of places; eat, drink
The toils of emp'rics, and their boasted practice;
Tincture of pearl, and coral, gold, and amber;
Be seen at feasts, and triumphs; have it asked,
What miracle she is? Set all the eyes
Of court afire, like a burning glass,
And work 'em into cinders; when the jewels

117–18 *I will rear . . . styles* I will see that this beauty becomes the type of all fashion
122 *mastery* the *magesterium* or master-work
131 *the Friars* Blackfriars
134 *Hundred* a subdivision of a county
136 *The toils of emp'rics* the products of experimental endeavour

Of twenty states adorn thee; and the light
Strikes out the stars; that, when thy name is mentioned,
Queens may look pale: and, we but showing our love,
Nero's Poppæa may be lost in story!
Thus, will we have it.

DOL
I could well consent, sir.
But, in a monarchy, how will this be?
The Prince will soon take notice; and both seize
You, and your stone: it being a wealth unfit
For any private subject.

MAMMON
If he knew it.

DOL
Yourself do boast it, sir.

MAMMON
To thee, my life.

DOL
O, but beware, sir! You may come to end
The remnant of your days, in a loathed prison,
By speaking of it.

MAMMON
'Tis no idle fear!
We'll therefore go with all, my girl, and live
In a free state; where we will eat our mullets,
Soused in high-country wines, sup pheasants' eggs,
And have our cockles, boiled in silver shells,
Our shrimps to swim again, as when they lived,
In a rare butter, made of dolphins' milk,
Whose cream does look like opals: and, with these
Delicate meats, set ourselves high for pleasure,
And take us down again, and then renew
Our youth, and strength, with drinking the elixir,
And so enjoy a perpetuity
Of life, and lust. And, thou shalt ha' thy wardrobe,
Richer than Nature's, still, to change thyself,

145 *Nero's Poppæa* so desired by Nero that he had her husband and his own wife killed in order to possess her. But she died of a kick from Nero (a typical *lapsus* on Mammon's part). Her beauty – and her solicitude for it – were legendary. She is supposed to have kept 500 asses in order to be able to bathe daily in their milk *story* history

157 *high-country wines* wines from hill country; but 'high' also suggests their intoxicating effect

160 *rare butter* as Geoffrey Hill remarks, this obvious oxymoron 'is a good, serious joke' (*The Lords of Limit*, London, 1984, p. 51)

166 *lust* both pleasure in general (the German *lust*) and sexual pleasure in particular. It is one of the Deadly Sins

167 *Richer than Nature's* see I.iv.27 n.; Shakespeare's Perdita would have considered such an attempt to outdo nature overweening and wrong

And vary oftener, for thy pride, than she:
Or Art, her wise, and almost equal servant.

[*Enter* FACE]

FACE
Sir, you are too loud. I hear you, every word,
Into the laboratory. Some fitter place.
The garden, or great chamber above. How like you her?

MAMMON
Excellent! Lungs. There's for thee. [*Gives money*]

FACE
But, do you hear?
Good sir, beware, no mention of the Rabbins.

MAMMON
We think not on 'em.

FACE
O, it is well, sir.
[*Exeunt* DOL, MAMMON]
Subtle!

Act IV, Scene ii

[*Enter*] SUBTLE [*to* FACE]

FACE
Dost thou not laugh?

SUBTLE
Yes. Are they gone?

FACE
All's clear.

SUBTLE
The widow is come.

FACE
And your quarrelling disciple?

SUBTLE
Ay.

FACE
I must to my Captainship again, then.

SUBTLE
Stay, bring 'em in, first.

FACE
So I meant. What is she?
A bonnibell?

SUBTLE
I know not.

FACE
We'll draw lots,
You'll stand to that?

168 *for thy pride* for your adornment
174 *Rabbins* rabbis; Hugh Broughton, from whose work Dol is to quote copiously, was expert in Judaic history and law
5 *bonnibell* (Fr.) 'bonne et belle', i.e. a good and pretty woman

SUBTLE
What else?

FACE
O, for a suit,
To fall now, like a curtain: flap.

SUBTLE
To th' door, man.

FACE
You'll ha' the first kiss, 'cause I am not ready.
[*Exit* FACE]

SUBTLE
Yes, and perhaps hit you through both the nostrils.

FACE [*within*]
Who would you speak with?

KASTRIL [*within*]
Where's the Captain?

FACE
Gone, sir.
About some business.

KASTRIL
Gone?

FACE
He'll return straight.
But master Doctor, his lieutenant, is here.

[*Enter* KASTRIL, DAME PLIANT, *Exit* FACE]

SUBTLE
Come near, my worshipful boy, my *terrae fili*,
That is, my boy of land; make thy approaches:
Welcome, I know thy lusts, and thy desires,
And I will serve, and satisfy 'em. Begin,
Charge me from thence, or thence, or in this line;
Here is my centre: ground thy quarrel.

KASTRIL
You lie.

SUBTLE
How, child of wrath, and anger! The loud lie?
For what, my sudden boy?

KASTRIL
Nay, that look you to,
I am aforehand.

SUBTLE
O, this 's no true grammar,
And as ill logic! You must render causes, child,
Your first, and second intentions, know your canons,
And your divisions, moods, degrees, and differences,
Your predicaments, substance, and accident,
Series extern, and intern, with their causes
Efficient, material, formal, final,
And ha' your elements perfect—

7 *suit* of clothes; Face needs to change into his captain's outfit
9 *hit . . . nostrils* 'lead you through the nose'
13 *terrae fili* (Lat.) son of the soil
17 *charge* accuse; attack 18 *ground* establish
22–8 *You must . . . perfect* Subtle applies the distinctions of logic to the art of quarrelling

KASTRIL What is this!
The angry tongue he talks in?
SUBTLE That false precept,
Of being aforehand, has deceived a number;
And made 'em enter quarrels, oftentimes,
Before they were aware: and, afterward,
Against their wills.
KASTRIL How must I do then, sir?
SUBTLE
I cry this lady mercy. She should, first,
Have been saluted. I do call you lady,
Because you are to be one, ere 't be long,

He kisses her

My soft, and buxom widow.
KASTRIL Is she, i'faith?
SUBTLE
Yes, or my art is an egregious liar.
KASTRIL
How know you?
SUBTLE By inspection, on her forehead,
And subtlety of her lip, which must be tasted

He kisses her again

Often, to make a judgement. 'Slight, she melts
Like a myrobalan! Here is, yet, a line
In *rivo frontis*, tells me, he is no knight.
PLIANT
What is he then, sir?
SUBTLE Let me see your hand.
O, your *linea Fortunae* makes it plain;
And *stella* here, in *monte Veneris*:
But, most of all, *iunctura annularis*.
He is a soldier, or a man of art, lady:
But shall have some great honour, shortly.
PLIANT Brother,
He's a rare man, believe me!
KASTRIL Hold your peace.

[*Enter* FACE *dressed as Captain*]

Here comes the tother rare man. 'Save you Captain.

35 *saluted* kissed; greeted 42 *myrobalan* fruit, like a plum
43 *in rivo frontis* in the vein of the forehead
45 *linea Fortunae* line of Fortune
46 *stella . . . monte Veneris* star on the mount of Venus (at the base of the thumb)
47 *iunctura annularis* joint of the ring finger

FACE
Good master Kastril. Is this your sister?

KASTRIL
Ay, sir.
Please you to kuss her, and be proud to know her?

FACE
I shall be proud to know you, lady.

PLIANT
Brother,
He calls me lady, too.

KASTRIL
Ay, peace. I heard it.

[FACE *and* SUBTLE *talk aside*]

FACE
The Count is come.

SUBTLE
Where is he?

FACE
At the door.

SUBTLE
Why, you must entertain him.

FACE
What'll you do
With these the while?

SUBTLE
Why, have 'em up, and show 'em
Some fustian book, or the dark glass.

FACE
'Fore God,
She is a delicate dab-chick! I must have her.

[*Exit* FACE]

SUBTLE
Must you? Ay, if your fortune will, you must.
[*To* KASTRIL] Come sir, the Captain will come to us presently.
I'll ha' you to my chamber of demonstrations,
Where I'll show you both the grammar, and logic,
And rhetoric of quarrelling; my whole method,
Drawn out in tables; and my instrument,
That hath the several scale upon't, shall make you
Able to quarrel, at a straw's breadth, by moonlight.
And, lady, I'll have you look in a glass,
Some half an hour, but to clear your eyesight,
Against you see your fortune: which is greater,
Than I may judge upon the sudden, trust me.

[*Exeunt* SUBTLE, KASTRIL, PLIANT]

53 *kuss* kiss (Kastril also says 'suster')
59 *fustian* written in jargon or cant
dark glass crystal ball
66 *Drawn out in tables* tabulated
71 *Against* in order that

Act IV, Scene iii

[*Enter*] FACE

FACE
Where are you, Doctor?
SUBTLE [*within*] I'll come to you presently.
FACE
I will ha' this same widow, now I ha' seen her,
On any composition.

[*Enter* SUBTLE]

SUBTLE What do you say?
FACE
Ha' you disposed of them?
SUBTLE I ha' sent 'em up.
FACE
Subtle, in troth, I needs must have this widow.
SUBTLE
Is that the matter?
FACE Nay, but hear me.
SUBTLE Go to,
If you rebel once, Dol shall know it all.
Therefore be quiet, and obey your chance.
FACE
Nay, thou art so violent now - Do but conceive:
Thou art old, and canst not serve—
SUBTLE Who, cannot I?
'Slight, I will serve her with thee, for a—
FACE Nay,
But understand: I'll gi' you composition.
SUBTLE
I will not treat with thee: what, sell my fortune?
'Tis better than my birthright. Do not murmur.
Win her, and carry her. If you grumble, Dol
Knows it directly.
FACE Well sir, I am silent.
Will you go help, to fetch in Don, in state? [*Exit* FACE]

11 *'Slight* 'Sblood Q

---

3 *composition* deal
10 *serve* a pun on the sense 'inseminate' (which adds a further dimension to 'conceive' in the previous line) 13 *treat* bargain

SUBTLE
I follow you, sir: we must keep Face in awe,
Or he will overlook us like a tyrant.

[*Enter* FACE,] SURLY *like a Spaniard*

Brain of a tailor! Who comes here? Don John!

SURLY
Señores, beso las manos, á vuestras mercedes.

SUBTLE
Would you had stooped a little, and kissed our *anos.*

FACE
Peace Subtle.

SUBTLE Stab me; I shall never hold, man.
He looks in that deep ruff, like a head in a platter,
Served in by a short cloak upon two trestles!

FACE
Or, what do you say to a collar of brawn, cut down
Beneath the souse, and wriggled with a knife?

SUBTLE
'Slud, he does look too fat to be a Spaniard.

FACE
Perhaps some Fleming, or some Hollander got him
In d'Alva's time: Count Egmont's bastard.

SUBTLE Don,
Your scurvy, yellow, Madrid face is welcome.

SURLY
Gratia.

SUBTLE He speaks, out of a fortification.

19 *overlook* look over; lord it over

20 *Don John* a common type-name for a Spaniard (like Mañuel now)

21 *Senores . . . mercedes* 'Gentlemen, I kiss your worships' hands'

24–5 *He looks . . . trestles* cf. John Webster, *The White Devil*, 'He carries his face in's ruff, as I have seen a serving-man carry glasses in a cypress hat-band, monstrous steady, for fear of breaking' (III.i.75–7)

27 *souse* ear

wriggled i.e. the knife has cut a zigzag pattern in the meat so that it looks pleated or folded like a ruff

30 *d'Alva* Fernando Alvarez, Duke of Alva, governor of the Spanish Netherlands between 1567 and 1573

Count Egmont a Flemish patriot executed by d'Alva in 1568

32 *Gratia* thank you

32–3 *He speaks . . . sets* Surly is immured in his ruff and the pleats resemble the crenellations of a fortress which could conceal explosives (squibs) in its recesses. The tubular pattern of the ruff's edge would itself evoke gun-barrels pointing outward from embrasures

Pray God, he ha' no squibs in those deep sets.

SURLY
Por Dios, Señores, muy linda casa!

SUBTLE
What says he?

FACE Praises the house, I think,
I know no more but's action.

SUBTLE Yes, the *casa*,
My precious Diego, will prove fair enough,
To cozen you in. Do you mark? You shall
Be cozened, Diego.

FACE Cozened, do you see?
My worthy Donzel, cozened.

SURLY *Entiendo.*

SUBTLE
Do you intend it? So do we, dear Don.
Have you brought pistolets? Or portagues?

He feels his pockets

My solemn Don? [*To* FACE] Dost thou feel any?

FACE [*To* SUBTLE] Full.

SUBTLE
You shall be emptied, Don; pumped, and drawn,
Dry, as they say.

FACE Milked, in troth, sweet Don.

SUBTLE
See all the monsters; the great lion of all, Don.

SURLY
Con licencia, se puede ver á esta señora?

SUBTLE
What talks he now?

FACE O' the *Señora.*

SUBTLE O, Don,
That is the lioness, which you shall see
Also, my Don.

34 *Por Dios . . . casa* 'By God gentlemen, a most charming house'
40 *Donzel* little Don
Entiendo I understand
46 *monsters . . . lion* lions were kept in the Tower of London as tourist attractions. Monsters (freaks and prodigies of various sorts) were also objects of holiday viewing
47 *Con . . . señora?* 'Is it possible, by your leave, to see the señora?'

FACE 'Slid, Subtle, how shall we do?
SUBTLE
For what?
FACE Why, Dol's employed, you know.
SUBTLE That's true!
'Fore heaven I know not: he must stay, that's all.
FACE
Stay? That he must not by no means.
SUBTLE No, why?
FACE
Unless you'll mar all. 'Slight, he'll suspect it.
And then he will not pay, not half so well.
This is a travelled punk-master, and does know
All the delays: a notable hot rascal,
And looks, already, rampant.
SUBTLE 'Sdeath, and Mammon
Must not be troubled.
FACE Mammon, in no case!
SUBTLE
What shall we do then?
FACE Think: you must be sudden.
SURLY
Entiendo, que la señora es tan hermosa, que codicio tan
á verla, como la bien aventuranza de mi vida.
FACE
Mi vida? 'Slid, Subtle, he puts me in mind o' the widow.
What dost thou say to draw her to't? Ha?
And tell her, it is her fortune. All our venture
Now lies upon 't. It is but one man more,
Which on's chance to have her: and, beside,
There is no maidenhead, to be feared, or lost.
What dost thou think on't, Subtle?
SUBTLE Who, I? Why—
FACE
The credit of our house too is engaged.
SUBTLE
You made me an offer for my share erewhile.
What wilt thou gi' me, i'faith?
FACE O, by that light,
I'll not buy now. You know your doom to me.
E'en take your lot, obey your chance, sir; win her,
And wear her, out for me.

60 *sudden* quick
61–2 *Entiendo ... vida* 'I understand that the señora is so beautiful that I long to see her as if she were my life's good fortune'

SUBTLE
'Slight. I'll not work her then.

FACE
It is the common cause, therefore bethink you.
Dol else must know it, as you said.

SUBTLE
I care not.

SURLY
Señores, porqué se tarda tanto?

SUBTLE
Faith, I am not fit, I am old.

FACE
That's now no reason, sir.

SURLY
Puede ser, de hacer burla de mi amor?

FACE
You hear the Don, too? By this air, I call.
And loose the hinges, Dol.

SUBTLE
A plague of hell—

FACE
Will you then do?

SUBTLE
You're a terrible rogue,
I'll think of this: will you, sir, call the widow?

FACE
Yes, and I'll take her too, with all her faults,
Now I do think on't better.

SUBTLE
With all my heart, sir,
Am I discharged o' the lot?

FACE
As you please.

SUBTLE
Hands.
[*They shake hands*]

FACE
Remember now, that upon any change,
You never claim her.

SUBTLE
Much good joy, and health to you, sir.
Marry a whore? Fate, let me wed a witch first.

SURLY
Por estas honradas barbas—

SUBTLE
He swears by his beard.
Dispatch, and call the brother too. [*Exit* FACE]

SURLY
Tengo dúda Señores,
Que no me hágan alguna traición.

78 *Senores . . . tanta?* 'Gentlemen, why so much delay?'
80 *Puede . . . amor* 'Perhaps you are treating my love as a joke?'
82 *loose the hinges* break our bond
91 *Por . . . barbas* 'By this honoured beard . . .'
92–3 *Tengo . . . traición* 'I suspect, gentlemen, that you are practising some kind of treachery on me'

SUBTLE
How, issue on? Yes, *praesto Señor*. Please you
Enthratha the *chambratha*, worthy Don;
Where if it please the Fates, in your *bathada*,
You shall be soaked, and stroked, and tubbed, and rubbed:
And scrubbed, and fubbed, dear Don, before you go.
You shall, in faith, my scurvy baboon Don:
Be curried, clawed, and flawed, and tawed, indeed.
I will the heartilier go about it now,
And make the widow a punk, so much the sooner,
To be revenged on this impetuous Face:
The quickly doing of it is the grace.
[*Exeunt* SUBTLE, SURLY]

Act IV, Scene iv

[*Enter*] FACE, KASTRIL, DAME PLIANT

FACE
Come lady: I knew, the Doctor would not leave,
Till he had found the very nick of her fortune.

KASTRIL
To be a Countess, say you?

FACE
A Spanish Countess, sir.

PLIANT
Why? Is that better than an English countess?

FACE
Better? 'Slight, make you that a question, lady?

KASTRIL
Nay, she is a fool, Captain, you must pardon her.

FACE
Ask from your courtier, to your Inns of Court-man,
To your mere milliner: they will tell you all,
Your Spanish jennet is the best horse. Your Spanish
Stoop is the best garb. Your Spanish beard

3 FACE Q; not in F

---

100 *curried* tickled; rubbed down (as in 'curry comb')
flawed flayed
tawed beaten (like leather being made pliable for use)
2 *nick* hiding place
9 *jennet* small Spanish horse
10 *Stoop* bow

Is the best cut. Your Spanish ruffs are the best
Wear. Your Spanish pavan the best dance.
Your Spanish titillation in a glove
The best perfume. And, for your Spanish pike,
And Spanish blade, let your poor Captain speak.
Here comes the Doctor.

[*Enter* SUBTLE]

SUBTLE My most honoured lady,
(For so I am now to style you, having found
By this my scheme, you are to undergo
All honourable fortune, very shortly.)
What will you say now, if some—

FACE I ha' told her all, sir.
And her right worshipful brother, here, that she shall be
A Countess: do not delay 'em, sir. A Spanish Countess.

SUBTLE
Still, my scarce worshipful Captain, you can keep
No secret. Well, since he has told you, madame,
Do you forgive him, and I do.

KASTRIL She shall do that, sir.
I'll look to't, 'tis my charge.

SUBTLE Well then. Nought rests
But that she fit her love, now, to her fortune.

PLIANT
Truly, I shall never brook a Spaniard.

SUBTLE No?

PLIANT
Never, sin' eighty-eight could I abide 'em,
And that was some three year afore I was born, in truth.

SUBTLE
Come, you must love him, or be miserable:
Choose, which you will.

FACE By this good rush, persuade her,

12 *pavan* a stately dance, introduced into England in the 16th century
13 *titillation* means of titillating – in this case scent
14–15 *pike . . . blade* Toledo is still famous for its steel. The vogue for things Spanish at court was due to James' desire for a closer link with Spain
18 *scheme* planetary chart
undergo there is a sexual innuendo here
29 *eighty-eight* 1588, the year of the Armada. Dame Pliant's voice is typical of popular anti-Spanish sentiment of the time
30 which makes Dame Pliant nineteen
32 *rush* rushes were used as floor cover in houses and on theatre stages

She will cry strawberries else, within this twelvemonth.

SUBTLE

Nay, shads, and mackerel, which is worse.

FACE

Indeed, sir?

KASTRIL

God's lid, you shall love him, or I'll kick you.

PLIANT

Why?

I'll do as you will ha' me, brother.

KASTRIL

Do,

Or by this hand, I'll maul you.

FACE

Nay, good sir,

Be not so fierce.

SUBTLE

No, my enraged child,

She will be ruled. What, when she comes to taste

The pleasure of a Countess! To be courted—

FACE

And kissed, and ruffled!

SUBTLE

Ay, behind the hangings.

FACE

And then come forth in pomp!

SUBTLE

And know her state!

FACE

Of keeping all th'idolators o' the chamber

Barer to her, than at their prayers!

SUBTLE

Is served

Upon the knee!

FACE

And has her pages, ushers,

Footmen, and coaches—

SUBTLE

Her six mares—

FACE

Nay, eight!

SUBTLE

To hurry her through London, to th' Exchange,

33 *cry strawberries* become a street fruit vendor

34 *shads* a species of herring; Subtle suggests that it is worse to sell fish than fruit. 'Fish wife' is still a derogatory term

41 *behind the hangings* wall-hangings – like the arras in *Hamlet* – provided useful hiding-places in great houses

44 *Barer* of their hats (and perhaps more)

47 *th' Exchange* the New Exchange in the Strand – a fashionable meeting place where negotiations and purchases took place. It was opened in 1609

Bedlam, the China-houses—

FACE
Yes, and have
The citizens gape at her, and praise her tires!
And my lord's goose-turd bands, that rides with her!

KASTRIL
Most brave! By this hand, you are not my suster,
If you refuse.

PLIANT
I will not refuse, brother.

[*Enter* SURLY]

SURLY
Qué es esto, Señores, que no se venga?
Esta tardanza me mata!

FACE
It is the Count come!
The Doctor knew he would be here, by his art.

SUBTLE
En galanta madama, Don! Galantissima!

SURLY
Por todos los dioses, la más acabada
Hermosura, que he visto en mi vida!

FACE
Is't not a gallant language, that they speak?

KASTRIL
An admirable language! Is't not French?

FACE
No, Spanish, sir.

KASTRIL
It goes like law-French,
And that, they say, is the courtliest language.

FACE
List, sir.

48 *Bedlam* Bethlehem Royal Hospital for the insane. Viewing the inmates was considered a chic pastime
China-houses London shops where Oriental silks and porcelains were sold. These three places are also found grouped together as loci for fashionable living in *Epicoene*, IV.iii.24–5

49 *tires* attires

50 *goose-turd bands* collars of the fashionable goose-turd shade of green

53–4 *Qué . . . mata* 'Why doesn't she come, gentlemen? This delay is killing me'

56 *En . . . Galantissima!* Subtle speaks a made-up Spanglish: 'A fine woman, Don, very fine!'

57–8 *Por . . . vida!* 'By all the gods, the most perfect beauty that I have seen in [all] my life!'

61 *law-French* a very corrupt derivation of Norman French, still used in law-courts at the date of the play though discontinued soon after

62 *courtliest* in this case the language of the law courts rather than the royal court
List listen

SURLY
El sol ha perdido su lumbre, con el
Resplandor, que trae esta dama. Válgame dios!
FACE
He admires your sister.
KASTRIL Must not she make curtsey?
SUBTLE
'Ods will, she must go to him, man; and kiss him!
It is the Spanish fashion, for the women
To make first court.
FACE 'Tis true he tells you, sir:
His art knows all.
SURLY *Porqué no se acude?*
KASTRIL
He speaks to her, I think?
FACE That he does sir.
SURLY
Por el amor de dios, qué es esto, que se tarda?
KASTRIL
Nay, see: she will not understand him! Gull.
Noddy.
PLIANT What say you brother?
KASTRIL Ass, my suster,
Go kuss him, as the cunning man would ha' you,
I'll thrust a pin i' your buttocks else.
FACE O, no sir.
SURLY
Señora mía, mi persona muy indigna está
Á llegar á tanta hermosura.
FACE
Does he not use her bravely?
KASTRIL Bravely, i' faith!
FACE
Nay, he will use her better.
KASTRIL Do you think so?
SURLY
Señora, si sera servida, entremos.
[*Exeunt* SURLY, DAME PLIANT]

63–4 *El . . . Dios!* 'The sun has lost its light with the splendour that this lady bears, so help me God!'

69 *Porqué . . . acude?* 'Why doesn't she come?'

71 *Por . . . tarda?* 'For the love of God, what is it that makes her delay?'

76–7 *Señora . . . hermosura* 'My lady, my person is wholly unworthy to approach such beauty'

80 *Señora . . . entremos* 'Señora, if it is convenient, let us go in.' (There is a pun on 'serve' here)

KASTRIL
Where does he carry her?
FACE
Into the garden, sir;
Take you no thought: I must interpret for her.
SUBTLE
Give Dol the word [*Exit* FACE] Come, my fierce child, advance,
We'll to our quarrelling lesson again.
KASTRIL
Agreed.
I love a Spanish boy, with all my heart.
SUBTLE
Nay, and by this means, sir, you shall be brother
To a great Count.
KASTRIL
Ay, I knew that, at first.
This match will advance the house of the Kastrils.
SUBTLE
Pray God, your sister prove but pliant.
KASTRIL
Why,
Her name is so: by her other husband.
SUBTLE
How!
KASTRIL
The widow Pliant. Knew you not that?
SUBTLE
No faith, sir.
Yet, by erection of her figure, I guessed it.
Come, let's go practise.
KASTRIL
Yes, but do you think, Doctor,
I e'er shall quarrel well?
SUBTLE
I warrant you.
[*Exeunt* SUBTLE, KASTRIL]

Act IV, Scene v

[*Enter*] DOL *in her fit of talking*, MAMMON

DOL
For, after Alexander's death—

83 *the word* i.e. to begin her 'fit'
87 *great Count* an aural quibble on 'cunt'
92 *by erection of her figure* by the drawing of her horoscope. Subtle also suggests the erection which Dame Pliant's figure has aroused in him
1–32 *after . . . Rome* Dol's diatribe is a patchwork of quotations from Hugh Broughton's *A Concent of Scripture* (1590) which attempts to answer questions of Old Testament chronology

MAMMON Good lady—

DOL
That Perdiccas, and Antigonus were slain,
The two that stood, Seleuc', and Ptolomee—

MAMMON
Madam.

DOL Made up the two legs, and the fourth Beast.
That was Gog-north, and Egypt-south: which after
Was called Gog-Iron-leg, and South-Iron-leg—

MAMMON Lady—

DOL
And then Gog-horned. So was Egypt, too.
Then Egypt-clay-leg, and Gog-clay-leg—

MAMMON Sweet madam.

DOL
And last God-dust, and Egypt-dust, which fall
In the last link of the fourth chain. And these
Be stars in story, which none see, or look at—

MAMMON
What shall I do?

DOL For, as he says, except
We call the Rabbins, and the heathen Greeks—

MAMMON
Dear lady.

DOL To come from Salem, and from Athens,
And teach the people of Great Britain—

[*Enter* FACE *dressed as bellows-man*]

FACE What's the matter, sir?

DOL
To speak the tongue of Eber, and Javan—

MAMMON O,
She's in her fit.

DOL We shall know nothing—

FACE Death, sir,
We are undone.

2–3 *Perdicas . . . Antigonus . . . Seleuc' . . . Ptolomee* the four generals of Alexander the Great, recipients of his divided empire. Alexander's empire was interpreted as one of the 'four kingdoms' mentioned by Daniel in his interpretation of Nebuchadnezzar's dream

10 *the fourth chain* 'Fiue, as it were, chaines of time are in Scripture . . . the fourth chaine containeth the continuance of Nebuchadnezar's 70 yeares', Broughton, *Daniel his Chaldie Visions and his Ebrew*, London, 1596, Hijv

14 *Salem* Jerusalem

16 *Eber, and Javan* Hebrew and Gentile tongues

DOL Where, then, a learned linguist
Shall see the ancient used communion
Of vowels, and consonants—

FACE My master will hear!

DOL
A wisdom, which Pythagoras held most high—

MAMMON
Sweet honourable lady.

DOL To comprise
All sounds of voices, in few marks of letters—

FACE
Nay, you must never hope to lay her now.

They speak together

DOL
And so we may arrive by Talmud skill,
And profane Greek, to raise the building up
Of Helen's house, against the Ismaelite,
King of Thogarma, and his habergeons
Brimstony, blue, and fiery; and the force
Of King Abaddon, and the Beast of Cittim:
Which Rabbi David Kimchi, Onkelos,
And Aben-Ezra do interpret Rome.

FACE
How did you put her into't?

MAMMON Alas I talked
Of a fifth monarchy I would erect,
With the philosopher's stone (by chance) and she
Falls on the other four, straight. FACE Out of Broughton!
I told you so. 'Slid stop her mouth. MAMMON Is't best?

FACE
She'll never leave else. If the old man hear her,
We are but fæces, ashes.

SUBTLE [*within*] What's to do there?

FACE
O, we are lost. Now she hears him, she is quiet.

25, 29 MAMMON MAN. F
27 *With the* Which the Q

---

25 *Talmud* the great rabbinical thesaurus
26 *fifth monarchy* the millenium; identified with the 'stone ... cut out of the mountain without hands ... that ... brake in pieces the iron, the brass, the clay, the silver and the gold' of *Daniel* ii.45 – the fifth kingdom which will destroy the other four imaged by the clay-footed statue of Nebuchadnezzar's dream

Upon SUBTLE'*s entry they disperse*
[*Exeunt* DOL *and* FACE]

MAMMON
Where shall I hide me?
SUBTLE
How! What sight is here!
Close deeds of darkness, and that shun the light!
Bring him again. Who is he? What, my son!
O, I have lived too long.
MAMMON
Nay good, dear Father,
There was no unchaste purpose.
SUBTLE
Not? And flee me,
When I come in?
MAMMON
That was my error.
SUBTLE
Error?
Guilt, guilt, my son. Give it the right name. No marvel,
If I found check in our great work within,
When such affairs as these were managing!
MAMMON
Why, have you so?
SUBTLE
It has stood still this half hour:
And all the rest of our less works gone back.
Where is the instrument of wickedness,
My lewd false drudge?
MAMMON
Nay, good sir, blame not him.
Believe me, 'twas against his will, or knowledge.
I saw her by chance.
SUBTLE
Will you commit more sin,
T'excuse a varlet?
MAMMON
By my hope, 'tis true, sir.
SUBTLE
Nay, then I wonder less, if you, for whom
The blessing was prepared, would so tempt heaven:
And lose your fortunes.
MAMMON
Why, sir?
SUBTLE
This'll retard
The work, a month at least.
MAMMON
Why, if it do,
What remedy? But think it not, good Father:
Our purposes were honest.

42 *stood still* gone back Q
43 *gone back* stand still Q
51 *This'll retard* This will hinder Q

---

41 *managing* taking place

SUBTLE As they were,
So the reward will prove.

A great crack and noise within

How now! Ay me.
God, and all saints be good to us. What's that?

[*Enter* FACE]

FACE
O sir, we are defeated! All the works
Are flown *in fumo*: every glass is burst.
Furnace, and all rent down! As if a bolt
Of thunder had been driven through the house.
Retorts, receivers, pelicans, boltheads,
All struck in shivers!

SUBTLE *falls down as in a swoon*

Help, good, sir! Alas,
Coldness, and death invades him. Nay, sir Mammon,
Do the fair offices of a man! You stand,
As you were readier to depart, than he.

One knocks

Who's there? My lord her brother is come.

MAMMON Ha, Lungs?

FACE
His coach is at the door. Avoid his sight,
For he's as furious, as his sister is mad.

MAMMON
Alas!

FACE My brain is quite undone with the fume, sir,
I ne'er must hope to be mine own man again.

MAMMON
Is all lost, Lungs? Will nothing be preserved,
Of all our cost?

FACE Faith, very little, sir.
A peck of coals, or so, which is cold comfort, sir.

MAMMON
O my voluptuous mind! I am justly punished.

FACE
And so am I, sir.

MAMMON Cast from all my hopes—

FACE
Nay, certainties, sir.

58 *in fumo* in smoke
61 *receivers* vessels used to retain distillates

MAMMON By mine own base affections.

SUBTLE *seems to come to himself*

SUBTLE
O, the curst fruits of vice, and lust!

MAMMON Good father,
It was my sin. Forgive it.

SUBTLE Hangs my roof
Over us still, and will not fall, O justice,
Upon us, for this wicked man!

FACE Nay, look, sir,
You grieve him, now, with staying in his sight:
Good sir, the nobleman will come too, and take you,
And that may breed a tragedy.

MAMMON I'll go.

FACE
Ay, and repent at home, sir. It may be,
For some good penance, you may ha' it, yet,
A hundred pound to the box at Bedlam—

MAMMON Yes.

FACE
For the restoring such as ha' their wits.

MAMMON I'll do't.

FACE
I'll send one to you to receive it.

MAMMON Do.
Is no projection left?

FACE All flown, or stinks, sir.

MAMMON
Will nought be saved, that's good for med'cine, thinkst thou?

FACE
I cannot tell, sir. There will be, perhaps,
Something, about the scraping of the shards,
Will cure the itch: though not your itch of mind, sir.
It shall be saved for you, and sent home. Good sir,
This way: for fear the lord should meet you.

[*Exit* MAMMON]

SUBTLE Face.

FACE
Ay.

SUBTLE Is he gone?

86 *box* charity collection box
93 *itch* a contagious pustular disease in which the skin is inflamed and itchy

FACE Yes, and as heavily
As all the gold he hoped for, were in his blood.
Let us be light, though.

SUBTLE Ay, as balls, and bound
And hit our heads against the roof for joy:
There's so much of our care now cast away.

FACE
Now to our Don.

SUBTLE Yes, your young widow, by this time
Is made a Countess, Face: she's been in travail
Of a young heir for you.

FACE Good, sir.

SUBTLE Off with your case,
And greet her kindly, as a bridegroom should,
After these common hazards.

FACE Very well, sir.
Will you go fetch Don Diego off, the while?

SUBTLE
And fetch him over too, if you'll be pleased, sir:
Would Dol were in her place, to pick his pockets now.

FACE
Why, you can do it as well, if you would set to't.
I pray you prove your virtue.

SUBTLE For your sake, sir.

[*Exeunt* SUBTLE *and* FACE]

Act IV, Scene vi

[*Enter*] SURLY, DAME PLIANT

SURLY
Lady, you see into what hands you are fall'n;
'Mongst what a nest of villians! And how near
Your honour was t'have catched a certain clap

98 *balls* bubbles
99–100 the final syllables of these lines would have rhymed in 17th-century pronunciation
102 *travail* labour
103 *case* disguise
106 *fetch . . . off* keep him away
107 *fetch . . . over* get one up on him
3 *clap* then, as now, gonorrhoea; but also used to mean any sudden stroke of misfortune

(Through your credulity) had I but been
So punctually forward, as place, time,
And other circumstance would ha' made a man:
For you're a handsome woman: would y'were wise, too.
I am a gentleman, come here disguised,
Only to find the knaveries of this citadel,
And where I might have wronged your honour, and have
not,
I claim some interest in your love. You are,
They say, a widow, rich: and I am a bachelor,
Worth nought: your fortunes may make me a man,
As mine ha' preserved you a woman. Think upon it,
And whether, I have deserved you, or no.

PLIANT I will, sir.

SURLY
And for these household-rogues, let me alone,
To treat with them.

[*Enter* SUBTLE]

SUBTLE How doth my noble Diego?
And my dear madam, Countess? Hath the Count
Been courteous, lady? Liberal? And open?
Donzell, methinks you look melancholic,
After your *coitum*, and scurvy! Truly,
I do not like the dulness of your eye:
It hath a heavy cast, 'tis upsee Dutch,
And says you are a lumpish whore-master,
Be lighter, I will make your pockets so.

He falls to picking of them

SURLY
Will you, Don bawd, and pickpurse? How now?
[*Sets on him*]
Reel you?
Stand up sir, you shall find since I am so heavy,
I'll gi' you equal weight.

SUBTLE Help, murder!

SURLY No, sir.
There's no such thing intended. A good cart,
And a clean whip shall ease you of that fear.

16 SURLY SVB. F

---

23 *upsee Dutch* from the Dutch *op zijn*: 'to be up'; i.e. a drinking term like 'bottoms up'; here the phrase probably means something like 'drunk as a Dutchman'

29–30 *cart . . . whip* to be whipped behind a cart was a common public punishment for prostitutes

I am the Spanish Don, that should be cozened,
Do you see? Cozened? Where's your Captain Face?
That parcel-broker, and whole-bawd, all rascal.

[*Enter* FACE *dressed as Captain*]

FACE
How, Surly!
SURLY O, make your approach, good Captain.
I have found, from whence your copper rings, and spoons
Come now, wherewith you cheat abroad in taverns.
'Twas here, you learned t'anoint your boot with brimstone,
Then rub men's gold on't, for a kind of touch,
And say 'twas naught, when you had changed the colour,
That you might ha't for nothing? And this Doctor,
Your sooty, smoky-bearded compeer, he
Will close you so much gold, in a bolt's head,
And, on a turn, convey (i' the stead) another
With sublimed mercury, that shall burst i' the heat,
And fly out all *in fumo*? Then weeps Mammon:
Then swoons his worship. Or, he is the Faustus,
[FACE *slips out*]
That casteth figures, and can conjure, cures
Plague, piles, and pox, by the ephemerides,
And holds intelligence with all the bawds,
And midwives of three shires? While you send in—
Captain, (what is he gone?) damsels with child,
Wives, that are barren, or, the waiting-maid
With the green sickness? [SUBTLE *attempts to leave*]
Nay, sir, you must tarry
Though he be 'scaped; and answer, by the ears, sir.

33 *parcel-broker* part-broker; 'broker' means 'pawnbroker'; probably a receiver of stolen goods

37–9 *anoint . . . colour* gold was tested by being rubbed against touchstone on which it left a trace whose quality could be analysed

40–5 *Doctor . . . in fumo* a trick by which the fraudulent alchemist pockets the gold (in a bolt's head) and replaces it with a similar container holding mercury which will then explode and give the appearance of the gold being lost in smoke

41 *compeer* colleague

46 *Faustus* Johann Faustus, the damned necromancer hero of Marlowe's *Doctor Faustus*

48 *ephemerides* an almanac indicating planetary positions for astrological use

53 *green sickness* an anaemic disease to which pubertal women are susceptible

54 *by the ears* see I.i.169

Act IV, Scene vii

[*Enter*] FACE, KASTRIL [*to them*]

FACE
Why, now's the time, if ever you will quarrel
Well (as they say) and be a true-born child.
The Doctor, and your sister both are abused.

KASTRIL
Where is he? Which is he? He is a slave
Whate'er he is, and the son of a whore. Are you
The man, sir, I would know?

SURLY
I should be loath, sir,
To confess so much.

KASTRIL
Then you lie, i' your throat.

SURLY
How?

FACE
A very errant rogue, sir, and a cheater,
Employed here, by another conjurer,
That does not love the Doctor, and would cross him
If he knew how—

SURLY
Sir, you are abused.

KASTRIL
You lie:
And 'tis no matter.

FACE
Well said, sir. He is
The impudentest rascal—

SURLY
You are indeed. Will you hear me, sir?

FACE
By no means: bid him be gone.

KASTRIL
Be gone, sir, quickly.

SURLY
This's strange! Lady, do you inform your brother.

FACE
There is not such a foist, in all the town,
The Doctor had him, presently: and finds, yet,
The Spanish Count will come, here. Bear up, Subtle.

SUBTLE
Yes, sir, he must appear, within this hour.

FACE
And yet this rogue, would come, in a disguise,

2 *child* the sense 'nobly born' was still current
16 *foist* cheat, rogue

By the temptation of another spirit,
To trouble our art, though he could not hurt it.

KASTRIL
Ay,
I know – Away, you talk like a foolish mauther.

[*Exit* DAME PLIANT]

SURLY
Sir, all is truth, she says.

FACE
Do not believe him, sir:
He is the lyingest swabber! Come your ways, sir.

SURLY
You are valiant, out of company.

KASTRIL
Yes, how then, sir?

[*Enter* DRUGGER]

Nay, here's an honest fellow too, that knows him,
And all his tricks. (Make good what I say, Abel,)
This cheater would ha' cozened thee o' the widow.
He owes this honest Drugger, here, seven pound,
He has had on him, in two-penny 'orths of tobacco.

DRUGGER
Yes sir. And he's damned himself, three terms, to pay me.

FACE
And what does he owe for *lotium*?

DRUGGER
Thirty shillings, sir:
And for six syringes.

SURLY
Hydra of villany!

FACE
Nay, sir, you must quarrel him out o' the house.

KASTRIL
I will.
Sir, if you get not out o' doors, you lie:
And you are a pimp.

SURLY
Why, this is madness, sir,
Not valour in you: I must laugh at this.

32 *he's* he hath Q

---

23 *mauther* young woman
25 *swabber* deck-hand
26 *out of* 'because you are in'
33 *lotium* stale urine used by barbers as a lye for the hair
34 *Hydra* a monster whose many heads multiplied each time one was severed – a fitting epithet for Face

KASTRIL
It is my humour: you are a pimp, and a trig,
And an Amadis de Gaul, or a Don Quixote.

DRUGGER
Or a Knight o' the Curious Coxcomb. Do you see?

[*Enter* ANANIAS]

ANANIAS
Peace to the household.

KASTRIL
I'll keep peace, for no man.

ANANIAS
Casting of dollars is concluded lawful.

KASTRIL
Is he the Constable?

SUBTLE
Peace, Ananias.

FACE
No, sir.

KASTRIL
Then you are an otter, and a shad, a whit,
A very tim.

SURLY
You'll hear me, sir?

KASTRIL
I will not.

ANANIAS
What is the motive?

SURLY
Zeal, in the young gentleman,
Against his Spanish slops—

ANANIAS
They are profane,
Lewd, superstitious, and idolatrous breeches.

SURLY
New rascals!

KASTRIL
Will you be gone, sir?

ANANIAS
Avoid Satan,
Thou art not of the light. That ruff of pride,

39 *trig* coxcomb

40 *Amadis de Gaul* the name of a Spanish or Portuguese romance written up by Garcia de Montalvo in the second half of the 15th century
Don Quixote eponymous hero of Cervantes' novel; the *Amadis de Gaul* is one of the few romances excused from burning in *Don Quixote*

41 *Knight o' the Curious Coxcomb* a reference to Surly's extraordinary headgear

45–6 *shad . . . whit . . . tim* the first of these is a small fish; the *OED* cites this passage in defining the other two as terms of abuse; they are Kastril's home-made insults; each has a diminutive sound

About thy neck, betrays thee: and is the same
With that, which the unclean birds, in seventy-seven,
Were seen to prank it with, on divers coasts.
Thou look'st like Antichrist, in that lewd hat.

SURLY
I must give way.

KASTRIL
Be gone, sir.

SURLY
But I'll take
A course with you—

ANANIAS
(Depart, proud Spanish fiend)

SURLY
Captain, and Doctor—

ANANIAS
Child of perdition.

KASTRIL
Hence, sir.
[*Exit* SURLY]
Did I not quarrel bravely?

FACE
Yes, indeed, sir.

KASTRIL
Nay, and I give my mind to't, I shall do't.

FACE
O, you must follow, sir, and threaten him tame.
He'll turn again else.

KASTRIL
I'll re-turn him, then.
[*Exit* KASTRIL]

FACE
Drugger, this rogue prevented us, for thee:
We had determined, that thou shouldst ha' come,
In a Spanish suit, and ha' carried her so; and he
A brokerly slave, goes, puts it on himself.
Hast brought the damask?

DRUGGER
Yes sir.

FACE
Thou must borrow,
A Spanish suit. Hast thou no credit with the players?

DRUGGER
Yes, sir, did you never see me play the fool?

52–4 *the same ... coasts* Malcolm H. South argues that the 'unclean birds' are Catholic seminary priests trained on the Continent and returned to England wearing outlandish ruffs. 'The Vncleane Birds, in Seuenty-Seven: *The Alchemist*' *Studies in English Literature 1500–1900*, xiii (1973), pp. 331–43

63 *prevented* forestalled

67–8 *borrow ... players* stage costumes were augmented by court cast-offs so actors might have a supply of the Spanish clothes in fashion at Court

69 *did you never see me play the fool?* an illusion-breaking joke: the part of Drugger would have been taken by the leading comic actor in the company – Robert Armin in the first instance

FACE
I know not, Nab: thou shalt, if I can help it.
Hieronymo's old cloak, ruff, and hat will serve,
I'll tell thee more, when thou bring'st 'em.
[*Exit* DRUGGER]

SUBTLE *hath whispered with him this while*

ANANIAS Sir, I know
The Spaniard hates the Brethren, and hath spies
Upon their actions: and that this was one
I make no scruple. But the holy Synod
Have been in prayer, and meditation, for it.
And 'tis revealed no less, to them, than me,
That casting of money is most lawful.
SUBTLE True.
But here, I cannot do it; if the house
Should chance to be suspected, all would out,
And we be locked up, in the Tower, forever,
To make gold there (for th' state) never come out:
And, then, are you defeated.
ANANIAS I will tell
This to the Elders, and the weaker Brethren,
That the whole company of the Separation
May join in humble prayer again.
SUBTLE (And fasting.)
ANANIAS
Yea, for some fitter place. The peace of mind
Rest with these walls.
SUBTLE Thanks, courteous Ananias.
[*Exit* ANANIAS]

FACE
What did he come for?
SUBTLE About casting dollars,
Presently, out of hand. And so, I told him,
A Spanish minister came here to spy,
Against the faithful—
FACE I conceive. Come Subtle,
Thou art so down upon the least disaster!
How wouldst th' ha' done, if I had not helped thee out?
SUBTLE
I thank thee Face, for the angry boy, i' faith.

71 *Hieronymo* the crazed, revenging hero of Kyd's *Spanish Tragedy*. It is possible that Jonson played this role

FACE
Who would ha' looked, it should ha' been that rascal?
Surly? He had dyed his beard, and all. Well, sir,
Here's damask come, to make you a suit.
SUBTLE
Where's Drugger?
FACE
He is gone to borrow me a Spanish habit,
I'll be the Count, now.
SUBTLE
But where's the widow?
FACE
Within, with my lord's sister: Madam Dol
Is entertaining her.
SUBTLE
By your favour, Face,
Now she is honest, I will stand again.
FACE
You will not offer it?
SUBTLE
Why?
FACE
Stand to your word,
Or—here comes Dol. She knows—
SUBTLE
You're tyrannous still.

[*Enter* DOL]

FACE
Strict for my right. How now, Dol? Hast told her,
The Spanish Count will come?
DOL
Yes, but another is come,
You little looked for!
FACE
Who's that?
DOL
Your master:
The master of the house.
SUBTLE
How, Dol!
FACE
She lies.
This is some trick. Come, leave your quiblins, Dorothy.
DOL
Look out, and see.
SUBTLE
Art thou in earnest?
DOL
'Slight,
Forty o' the neighbours are about him, talking.
FACE
'Tis he, by this good day.
DOL
'Twill prove ill day,

104 SUBTLE SVR. F

---

96 *looked* realised; thought
110 *quiblins* tricks

For some on us.

FACE
We are undone, and taken.

DOL
Lost, I am afraid.

SUBTLE
You said he would not come,
While there died one a week, within the liberties.

FACE
No: 'twas within the walls.

SUBTLE
Was't so? Cry you mercy:
I thought the liberties. What shall we do now, Face?

FACE
Be silent: not a word, if he call, or knock.
I'll into mine old shape again, and meet him,
Of Jeremy, the butler. I' the mean time,
Do you two pack up all the goods, and purchase,
That we can carry i' the two trunks. I'll keep him
Off for today, if I cannot longer: and then
At night, I'll ship you both away to Ratcliff,
Where we'll meet tomorrow, and there we'll share.
Let Mammon's brass, and pewter keep the cellar:
We'll have another time for that. But, Dol,
Pray thee, go heat a little water, quickly,
Subtle must shave me. All my Captain's beard
Must off, to make me appear smooth Jeremy.
You'll do't?

SUBTLE
Yes, I'll shave you, as well as I can.

FACE
And not cut my throat, but trim me?

SUBTLE
You shall see, sir.

[*Exeunt* SUBTLE, FACE, DOL]

126 *there* then Q

---

116 *liberties* the area surrounding a town subject to municipal authority
122 *purchase* gains
125 *Ratcliff* a riverside district of East London

Act V, Scene i

[In the street outside Lovewit's house]

[Enter] LOVEWIT, NEIGHBOURS

LOVEWIT
Has there been such resort, say you?
NEIGHBOUR 1 Daily, sir.
NEIGHBOUR 2
And nightly, too.
NEIGHBOUR 3 Ay, some as brave as lords.
NEIGHBOUR 4
Ladies, and gentlewomen.
NEIGHBOUR 5 Citizen's wives.
NEIGHBOUR 1
And knights.
NEIGHBOUR 6 In coaches.
NEIGHBOUR 2 Yes, and oyster-women.
NEIGHBOUR 1
Beside other gallants.
NEIGHBOUR 3 Sailors' wives.
NEIGHBOUR 4 Tobacco-men.
NEIGHBOUR 5
Another Pimlico!
LOVEWIT What should my knave advance,
To draw this company? He hung out no banners
Of a strange calf, with five legs, to be seen?
Or a huge lobster, with six claws?
NEIGHBOUR 6 No, sir.
NEIGHBOUR 3
We had gone in then, sir.
LOVEWIT He has no gift
Of teaching i' the nose, that e'er I knew of!

---

1 *resort* thronging of people

4 *oyster-women* female oyster sellers

6 *Pimlico* not the present Pimlico but a place in Hoxton (then Hogsden), east of the city, famous for pies and 'Pimlico' nut-brown ale
advance produce

8 *calf... legs* see *Bartholmew Fair*, V.iv.81–3, where this calf has matured to a bull. Such deformities were great money-spinners

11 *teaching i' the nose* i.e. with an impressive twang; la di da

You saw no bills set up, that promised cure
Of agues, or the toothache?

NEIGHBOUR 2 No such thing, sir.

LOVEWIT
Nor heard a drum struck, for baboons, or puppets?

NEIGHBOUR 5
Neither, sir.

LOVEWIT What device should he bring forth now!
I love a teeming wit, as I love my nourishment.
Pray God he ha' not kept such open house,
That he hath sold my hangings, and my bedding:
I left him nothing else. If he have eat 'em,
A plague o' the moth, say I. Sure he has got
Some bawdy pictures, to call all this ging;
The Friar, and the Nun; or the new motion
Of the Knight's courser, covering the Parson's mare;
The boy of six year old, with the great thing:
Or 't may be, he has the fleas that run at tilt,
Upon a table, or some dog to dance?
When saw you him?

NEIGHBOUR 1 Who sir, Jeremy?

NEIGHBOUR 2 Jeremy butler?
We saw him not this month.

LOVEWIT How!

NEIGHBOUR 4 Not these five weeks, sir.

NEIGHBOUR 1
These six weeks, at the least.

LOVEWIT Y' amaze me, neighbours!

NEIGHBOUR 5
Sure, if your worship know not where he is,
He's slipped away.

NEIGHBOUR 6 Pray God, he be not made away!

LOVEWIT
Ha? It's no time to question, then. *He knocks*

NEIGHBOUR 6 About
Some three weeks since, I heard a doleful cry,
As I sat up, a-mending my wife's stockings.

29 NEIGHBOUR 1 ed. Q, F omit 1

14 *drum struck* to 'drum up' a crowd 21 *ging* gang; crowd
22 *motion* puppet show
24 *The boy . . . thing* 'but of all the sights that ever were in London since I married, methinks the little child that was so fair grown about the members was the prettiest' Francis Beaumont, *The Knight of the Burning Pestle*, III.273–5
25 *at tilt* in a duel or tilting match

LOVEWIT
This's strange! That none will answer! Didst thou hear
A cry, saist thou?
NEIGHBOUR 6 Yes, sir, like unto a man
That had been strangled an hour, and could not speak.
NEIGHBOUR 2
I heard it too, just this day three weeks, at two o'clock
Next morning.
LOVEWIT These be miracles, or you make 'em so!
A man an hour strangled, and could not speak,
And both you heard him cry?
NEIGHBOUR 3 Yes, downward, sir.
LOVEWIT
Thou art a wise fellow: give me thy hand I pray thee.
What trade art thou on?
NEIGHBOUR 3 A smith, and't please your worship.
LOVEWIT
A smith? Then, lend me thy help, to get this door open.
NEIGHBOUR 3
That I will presently, sir, but fetch my tools—
[*Exit* NEIGHBOUR 3]
NEIGHBOUR 1
Sir, best to knock again, afore you break it.

Act V, Scene ii

LOVEWIT
I will. [*Knocks*]
[FACE, *clean-shaven as Jeremy, opens door*]
FACE What mean you, sir?
NEIGHBOURS 1, 2, 4 O, here's Jeremy!
FACE
Good sir, come from the door.
LOVEWIT Why! What's the matter?
FACE
Yet farther, you are too near, yet.
LOVEWIT I'the name of wonder!
What means the fellow?
FACE The house, sir, has been visited.

1 The trick used in this scene resembles the one played by the servant Tranio on his master Theropides in Plautus' *Mostellaria*

LOVEWIT
What? With the plague? Stand thou then farther.
FACE
No, sir,
I had it not.
LOVEWIT Who had it then? I left
None else, but thee, i'the house!
FACE
Yes, sir. My fellow,
The cat, that kept the buttery, had it on her
A week, before I spied it: but I got her
Conveyed away, i'the night. And so I shut
The house up for a month—
LOVEWIT
How!
FACE
Purposing then, sir,
T'have burnt rose-vinegar, treacle, and tar,
And, ha' made it sweet, that you should ne'er ha' known it:
Because I knew the news would but afflict you, sir.
LOVEWIT
Breathe less, and farther off. Why, this is stranger!
The neighbours tell me all, here, that the doors
Have still been open—
FACE
How, sir!
LOVEWIT
Gallants, men, and women,
And of all sorts, tag-rag, been seen to flock here
In threaves, these ten weeks, as to a second Hogsden,
In days of Pimlico, and Eye-bright!
FACE
Sir,
Their wisdoms will not say so!
LOVEWIT
Today, they speak
Of coaches, and gallants; one in a French hood,
Went in, they tell me: and another was seen
In a velvet gown, at the window! Divers more
Pass in and out!
FACE
They did pass through the doors then,
Or walls, I assure their eyesights, and their spectacles;
For here, sir, are the keys: and here have been,

24 *window* windore Q, F

19 *threaves* throngs
Hogsden Hoxton
20 *Eye-bright* a drinking place which made its name before Pimlico. *H.&S.* quote '*Pimlico. Or Runne Red-Cap: Eye-bright*, (so fam'd of late for *Beere*)/Although thy *Name* be numbered heere,/Thine ancient Honors now runne low;/Thou art struck blind by *Pimlyco*.' Perhaps its famous beer contained the herb Eyebright (*Euphrasia*)

In this my pocket, now, above twenty days!
And for before, I kept the fort alone, there.
But, that 'tis yet not deep i'the afternoon,
I should believe my neighbours had seen double
Through the black pot, and made these apparitions!
For, on my faith, to your worship, for these three weeks,
And upwards, the door has not been opened.

LOVEWIT
Strange!

NEIGHBOUR 1
Good faith, I think I saw a coach!

NEIGHBOUR 2
And I too,
I'd ha' been sworn!

LOVEWIT
Do you but think it now?
And but one coach?

NEIGHBOUR 4
We cannot tell, sir: Jeremy
Is a very honest fellow.

FACE
Did you see me at all?

NEIGHBOUR 1
No. That we are sure on.

NEIGHBOUR 2
I'll be sworn o' that.

LOVEWIT
Fine rogues, to have your testimonies built on!

[*Enter* NEIGHBOUR 3 *with his tools*]

NEIGHBOUR 3
Is Jeremy come?

NEIGHBOUR 1
O, yes, you may leave your tools,
We were deceived, he says.

NEIGHBOUR 2
He's had the keys:
And the door has been shut these three weeks.

NEIGHBOUR 3
Like enough.

LOVEWIT
Peace, and get hence, you changelings.

[*Enter* SURLY *and* MAMMON]

FACE
Surly come!
And Mammon made acquainted? They'll tell all.
(How shall I beat them off? What shall I do?)
Nothing's more wretched, than a guilty conscience.

42 NEIGHBOUR 1 MEI Q

---

32 *apparitions* the English title of Plautus' *Mostellaria* is *The Haunted House*
44 *changelings* those of unstable wits; so-called because they change their stories
47 *Mostellaria* 544: 'Nihil est miserius quam animus hominis conscius'

Act V, Scene iii

SURLY
No, sir, he was a great physician. This,
It was no bawdy-house: but a mere chancel.
You knew the lord, and his sister.

MAMMON
Nay, good Surly—

SURLY
The happy word, 'be rich'—

MAMMON
Play not the tyrant—

SURLY
Should be today pronounced, to all your friends.
And where be your andirons now? And your brass pots?
That should ha' been golden flagons, and great wedges?

MAMMON
Let me but breathe. What! They ha' shut their doors,
Me thinks! *MAMMON and SURLY knock*

SURLY Ay, now, 'tis holiday with them.

MAMMON
Rogues,
Cozeners, imposters, bawds.

FACE
What mean you, sir?

MAMMON
To enter if we can.

FACE
Another man's house?
Here is the owner, sir. Turn you to him,
And speak your business.

MAMMON
Are you, sir, the owner?

LOVEWIT
Yes, sir.

MAMMON And are those knaves, within, your cheaters?

LOVEWIT
What knaves? What cheaters?

MAMMON
Subtle, and his Lungs.

FACE
The gentleman is distracted, sir! No lungs,
Nor lights ha' been seen here these three weeks, sir,
Within these doors, upon my word!

SURLY
Your word,
Groom arrogant?

2 *chancel* the part of the church used for priestly offices
16 *distracted* out of his wits
16–17 *lungs . . . lights* puns on the anatomical sense of 'lights': entrails

FACE Yes, sir, I am the housekeeper,
And know the keys ha' not been out o' my hands.

SURLY
This's a new Face?

FACE You do mistake the house, sir!
What sign was't at?

SURLY You rascal! This is one
O' the confederacy. Come, let's get officers,
And force the door.

LOVEWIT Pray you stay, gentlemen.

SURLY
No, sir, we'll come with warrant.

MAMMON Ay, and then,
We shall ha' your doors open.

[*Exeunt* SURLY, MAMMON]

LOVEWIT What means this?

FACE
I cannot tell, sir!

NEIGHBOUR 1 These are two o' the gallants,
That we do think we saw.

FACE Two o' the fools?
You talk as idly as they. Good faith, sir,
I think the moon has crazed 'em all!

[*Enter* KASTRIL]

(O me,
The angry boy come too? He'll make a noise,
And ne'er away till he have betrayed us all.)

KASTRIL *knocks*

KASTRIL
What rogues, bawds, slaves, you'll open the door anon,
Punk, cockatrice, my suster. By this light
I'll fetch the marshal to you. You are a whore,
To keep your castle—

FACE Who would you speak with, sir?

KASTRIL
The bawdy Doctor, and the cozening Captain,
And Puss my suster.

LOVEWIT This is something, sure!

FACE
Upon my trust, the doors were never open, sir.

22 *sign* public eating houses, taverns and brothels all had signs like modern pub signs

30 *the moon* creator of lunacy

34 *cockatrice* a serpent, usually identified with the death-glancing Basilisk. Here it is used partly for its association with 'cock' (it was often used for prostitutes)

KASTRIL
I have heard all their tricks, told me twice over,
By the fat knight, and the lean gentleman.

LOVEWIT
Here comes another.

[*Enter* ANANIAS, TRIBULATION]

FACE Ananias too?
And his pastor?

TRIBULATION The doors are shut against us.

They beat too, at the door

ANANIAS
Come forth, you seed of sulphur, sons of fire,
Your stench, it is broke forth: abomination
Is in the house.

KASTRIL Ay, my suster's there.

ANANIAS The place,
It is become a cage of unclean birds.

KASTRIL
Yes, I will fetch the scavenger, and the constable.

TRIBULATION
You shall do well.

ANANIAS We'll join, to weed them out.

KASTRIL
You will not come then? Punk, device, my suster!

ANANIAS
Call her not sister. She is a harlot, verily.

KASTRIL
I'll raise the street.

LOVEWIT Good gentlemen, a word.

ANANIAS
Satan, avoid, and hinder not our zeal.

[*Exeunt* ANANIAS, TRIBULATION, KASTRIL]

LOVEWIT
The world's turned Bedlam.

44 *sulphur, sons of fire* Vipers, Sonnes of Belial Q
45 *stench, it* wickednesse Q
46 *Ay*, not in Q 48 *Yes* I (i.e. Ay) Q

---

47 *cage . . . birds* see IV.vii.53 and *Revelation* xviii.2
48 *scavenger* officer responsible for keeping streets clean and orderly
50 *Punk, device* perhaps by analogy with 'point-device' (faultlessly proper in dress). But 'device' may be an independent noun in his list of insults; in which case he is calling his sister a whore and a contraption
53 *avoid* clear off

FACE These are all broke loose,
Out of St. Katherine's, where they use to keep,
The better sort of mad folks.

NEIGHBOUR 1 All these persons
We saw go in, and out, here.

NEIGHBOUR 2 Yes, indeed, sir.

NEIGHBOUR 3
These were the parties.

FACE Peace, you drunkards. Sir,
I wonder at it! Please you, to give me leave
To touch the door, I'll try, and the lock be changed.

LOVEWIT
It mazes me!

FACE Good faith, sir, I believe,
There's no such thing. 'Tis all *deceptio visus*.
(Would I could get him away.)

DAPPER *cries out within*

DAPPER Master Captain, master Doctor.

LOVEWIT
Who's that?

FACE (Our clerk within, that I forgot!) I know not, sir.

DAPPER
For God's sake, when will her Grace be at leisure?

FACE Ha!
Illusions, some spirit o' the air: (his gag is melted,
And now he sets out the throat.)

DAPPER I am almost stifled—

FACE
(Would you were altogether.)

LOVEWIT 'Tis i' the house.
Ha! List.

FACE Believe it, sir, i' the air!

LOVEWIT Peace, you—

DAPPER
Mine aunt's Grace does not use me well.

SUBTLE [*within*] You fool,

55 *St. Katherine's* in fact the Hospital of St. Mary 'that was prouided for poore priests, and others, men and women in the City of London, that were fallen into frensie or losse of their memory' (Stow, ii, 143). This had been taken over by the Hospital of St. Katherine (on the north side of the Thames, just east of the Tower)

60 *and* either 'even if' or 'and see if'

62 *deceptio visus* an optical illusion

66 *sets out the throat* raises his voice

Peace, you'll mar all.

FACE
Or you will else, you rogue.

LOVEWIT
O, is it so? Then you converse with spirits!
Come sir. No more o' your tricks, good Jeremy,
The truth, the shortest way.

FACE
Dismiss this rabble, sir.
What shall I do? I am catched.

LOVEWIT
Good neighbours,
I thank you all. You may depart. [*Exeunt* NEIGHBOURS]
Come sir,
You know that I am an indulgent master:
And therefore, conceal nothing. What's your med'cine,
To draw so many several sorts of wild-fowl?

FACE
Sir, you were wont to affect mirth, and wit:
(But here's no place to talk on't i' the street.)
Give me but leave, to make the best of my fortune,
And only pardon me th'abuse of your house:
It's all I beg. I'll help you to a widow,
In recompense, that you shall gi' me thanks for,
Will make you seven years younger, and a rich one.
'Tis but your putting on a Spanish cloak,
I have her within. You need not fear the house,
It was not visited.

LOVEWIT
But by me, who came
Sooner than you expected.

FACE
It is true, sir.
'Pray you forgive me.

LOVEWIT
Well: let's see your widow.
[*Exeunt* LOVEWIT, FACE]

Act V, Scene iv

[*Inside Lovewit's house*]

[*Enter* SUBTLE, DAPPER]

SUBTLE
How! Ha' you eaten your gag?

DAPPER
Yes faith, it crumbled
Away i' my mouth.

SUBTLE
You ha' spoiled all then.

DAPPER
No,
I hope my aunt of Fairy will forgive me.

SUBTLE
Your aunt's a gracious lady: but in troth
You were to blame.
DAPPER
The fume did overcome me,
And I did do't to stay my stomach. 'Pray you
So satisfy her Grace. Here comes the Captain.

[*Enter* FACE]

FACE
How now! Is his mouth down?
SUBTLE
Ay! He has spoken!
FACE
(A pox, I heard him, and you too.) He's undone, then.
(I have been fain to say, the house is haunted
With spirits, to keep churl back.
SUBTLE
And hast thou done it?
FACE
Sure, for this night.
SUBTLE
Why, then triumph, and sing
Of Face so famous, the precious king
Of present wits.
FACE
Did you not hear the coil,
About the door?
SUBTLE
Yes, and I dwindled with it.)
FACE
Show him his aunt, and let him be dispatched:
I'll send her to you. [*Exit* FACE]
SUBTLE
Well sir, your aunt her Grace,
Will give you audience presently, on my suit,
And the Captain's word, that you did not eat your gag,
In any contempt of her Highness.
DAPPER
Not I, in troth, sir.

[*Enter*] DOL *like the Queen of Fairy*

SUBTLE
Here she is come. Down o' your knees, and wriggle:
She has a stately presence. Good. Yet nearer,
And bid, God save you.
DAPPER
Madam.
SUBTLE
And your aunt.

23 *you* her Q

---

7 S.D. *Enter* FACE who might now need a false beard since he was shaved at the end of Act IV (IV.vii.130–1)
8 *mouth down* gag gone
11 *churl* countryman
14 *coil* row

DAPPER
And my most gracious aunt, God save your Grace.
DOL
Nephew, we thought to have been angry with you:
But that sweet face of yours, hath turned the tide,
And made it flow with joy, that ebbed of love.
Arise, and touch our velvet gown.
SUBTLE
The skirts,
And kiss 'em. So.
DOL
Let me now stroke that head,
Much, nephew, shalt thou win; much shalt thou spend;
Much shalt thou give away: much shalt thou lend.
SUBTLE
(Ay, much, indeed.) Why do you not thank her Grace?
DAPPER
I cannot speak, for joy.
SUBTLE
See, the kind wretch!
Your Grace's kinsman right.
DOL
Give me the bird.
Here is your fly in a purse, about your neck, cousin,
Wear it, and feed it, about this day se'ennight,
On your right wrist—
SUBTLE
Open a vein, with a pin,
And let it suck but once a week: till then,
You must not look on't.
DOL
No. And, kinsman,
Bear yourself worthy of the blood you come on.
SUBTLE
Her Grace would ha' you eat no more Woolsack pies,
Nor Dagger frume'ty.
DOL
Nor break his fast,
In Heaven, and Hell.
SUBTLE
She's with you everywhere!
Nor play with costermongers, at mum-chance, tray-trip,
God-make-you-rich, (whenas your aunt has done it:) but keep

33 *kind* showing the affections of kin
34 *bird* Dapper's fly-familiar is a bird in fairyland
36 *se'ennight* week (seven nights)
41 *Woolsack pies* pies from the Woolsack tavern – probably the one outside Aldgate
42 *Dagger frume'ty* see I.i.191
43 *Heaven, and Hell* drinking places in Westminster, popular with lawyers' clerks. Hell had once been a debtor's prison
44 *mum-chance, tray-trip* dice games
45 *God-make-you-rich* a kind of backgammon

The gallantest company, and the best games—

DAPPER
Yes, sir.

SUBTLE
Gleek and primero: and what you get, be true to us.

DAPPER
By this hand, I will.

SUBTLE
You may bring's a thousand pound,
Before tomorrow night, (if but three thousand,
Be stirring) an' you will.

DAPPER
I swear, I will then.

SUBTLE
Your fly will learn you all games.

FACE [*within*]
Ha' you done there?

SUBTLE
Your grace will command him no more duties?

DOL
No:
But come, and see me often. I may chance
To leave him three or four hundred chests of treasure,
And some twelve thousand acres of Fairyland:
If he game well, and comely, with good gamesters.

SUBTLE
There's a kind aunt! Kiss her departing part.
But you must sell your forty mark a year, now:

DAPPER
Ay, sir, I mean.

SUBTLE
Or, gi't away: pox on't.

DAPPER
I'll gi't mine aunt. I'll go and fetch the writings.

SUBTLE
'Tis well, away. [*Exit* DAPPER]

[*Enter* FACE]

FACE
Where's Subtle?

SUBTLE
Here. What news?

FACE
Drugger is at the door, go take his suit,

50 *and* if Q
55 *twelve* fiue Q
58 *your* Q; you F
59 *pox* A pox Q
60 DAPPER FAC. Q, F

---

47 *Gleek and primero* see II.iii.284–5
50 *an' you will* should you feel like it
51 *learn* teach
56 *comely* (adv.) 'comelily'
57 *her departing part* i.e. her backside

And bid him fetch a parson, presently:
Say, he shall marry the widow. Thou shalt spend
A hundred pound by the service! [*Exit* SUBTLE]
Now, queen Dol,
Ha' you packed up all?

DOL
Yes.

FACE
And how do you like
The lady Pliant?

DOL
A good dull innocent.

[*Enter* SUBTLE]

SUBTLE
Here's your Hieronimo's cloak, and hat.

FACE
Give me 'em.

SUBTLE
And the ruff too?

FACE
Yes, I'll come to you presently.
[*Exit* FACE]

SUBTLE
Now, he is gone about his project, Dol,
I told you of, for the widow.

DOL
'Tis direct
Against our articles.

SUBTLE
Well, we'll fit him, wench.
Hast thou gulled her of her jewels, or her bracelets?

DOL
No, but I will do't.

SUBTLE
Soon at night, my Dolly,
When we are shipped, and all our goods aboard,
Eastward for Ratcliff; we will turn our course
To Brainford, westward, if thou saist the word:
And take our leaves of this o'erweening rascal,
This peremptory Face.

DOL
Content, I am weary of him.

SUBTLE
Th' hast cause, when the slave will run a-wiving, Dol,
Against the instrument, that was drawn between us.

DOL
I'll pluck his bird as bare as I can.

64 *spend* have to spend; i.e. gain
72 *articles* of faith (their 'venture tripartite', I.i.135)
77 *Brainford* Brentford, in Middlesex
81 *instrument* agreement

SUBTLE
Yes, tell her,
She must by any means, address some present
To th' cunning man; make him amends, for wronging
His art with her suspicion; send a ring;
Or chain of pearl; she will be tortured else
Extremely in her sleep, say: and ha' strange things
Come to her. Wilt thou?

DOL
Yes.

SUBTLE
My fine flitter-mouse,
My bird o'the night; we'll tickle it at the Pigeons,
When we have all, and may unlock the trunks,
And say, this's mine, and thine, and thine, and mine—

They kiss

[*Enter* FACE]

FACE
What now, a-billing?

SUBTLE
Yes, a little exalted
In the good passage of our stock-affairs.

FACE
Drugger has brought his parson, take him in, Subtle,
And send Nab back again, to wash his face.

SUBTLE
I will: and shave himself?

FACE
If you can get him. [*Exit* SUBTLE]

DOL
You are hot upon it, Face, what e'er it is!

FACE
A trick, that Dol shall spend ten pound a month by.

[*Enter* SUBTLE]

Is he gone?

SUBTLE
The chaplain waits you i'the hall, sir.

FACE
I'll go bestow him. [*Exit* FACE]

DOL
He'll now marry her, instantly.

95 *Nab* him Q

---

88 *flitter-mouse* bat
89 *tickle it* live it up
the Pigeons the Three Pigeons in Brentford market place (closed in 1916); John Lowin, the actor who played Mammon, kept it in the Commonwealth period
92 *a-billing* a pun for the audience who have witnessed Dol and Subtle tot up their gains
100 *bestow* conduct

SUBTLE
He cannot, yet, he is not ready. Dear Dol,
Cozen her of all thou canst. To deceive him
Is no deceit, but justice, that would break
Such an inextricable tie as ours was.

DOL
Let me alone to fit him.

[*Enter* FACE]

FACE Come, my venturers,
You ha' packed up all? Where be the trunks? Bring forth.

SUBTLE
Here.

FACE Let's see 'em. Where's the money?

SUBTLE Here,
In this.

FACE Mammon's ten pound: eight score before.
The Brethren's money, this. Drugger's, and Dapper's.
What paper's that?

DOL The jewel of the waiting maid's,
That stole it from her lady, to know certain—

FACE
If she should have precedence of her mistress?

DOL Yes.

FACE
What box is that?

SUBTLE The fish-wives' rings, I think:
And th' ale-wives' single money. Is't not Dol?

DOL
Yes: and the whistle, that the sailor's wife
Brought you, to know, and her husband were with Ward.

FACE
We'll wet it tomorrow: and our silver beakers,
And tavern cups. Where be the French petticoats,

102–4 *To deceive ... ours was* the word order is Latinate and confusing. A more usual order would be 'To deceive him that would break such an inextricable tie as ours was, is no deceit, but justice'

114 *single money* small change

116 *and* whether
Ward a notorious pirate. Andrew Barker, who had been made captive by him, published a pamphlet about his captor in 1609. Robert Daborne's play, *A Christian turn'd Turke: or the Tragicall Lives and Deaths of Two Famous Pyrates, Ward and Dansiker*, was acted in 1609 or 1610

117 *wet it* i.e. wet our whistles

And girdles, and hangers?
SUBTLE Here, i' the trunk,
And the bolts of lawn.
FACE Is Drugger's damask, there?
And the tobacco?
SUBTLE Yes.
FACE Give me the keys.
DOL
Why you the keys!
SUBTLE No matter, Dol: because
We shall not open 'em, before he comes.
FACE
'Tis true, you shall not open them, indeed:
Nor have 'em forth. Do you see? Not forth, Dol.
DOL No!
FACE
No, my smock-rampant. The right is, my master
Knows all, has pardoned me, and he will keep 'em.
Doctor, 'tis true (you look) for all your figures:
I sent for him, indeed. Wherefore, good partners,
Both he, and she, be satisfied: for, here
Determines the indenture tripartite,
Twixt Subtle, Dol, and Face. All I can do
Is to help you over the wall, o' the back-side;
Or lend you a sheet, to save your velvet gown, Dol.
Here will be officers, presently; bethink you,
Of some course suddenly to scape the dock:
For thither you'll come else. *Some knock*
SUBTLE Hark you, thunder.
You are a precious fiend!
OFFICERS [*without*] Open the door.
FACE
Dol, I am sorry for thee i' faith. But hearst thou?
It shall go hard, but I will place thee somewhere:

119 *hangars* loops on sword belts from which swords could be hung
120 *bolts* rolls
128 *for your figures* in spite of all your astrological charts; i.e. you never foresaw this
129 *I sent . . . indeed* not true; Face is trying to 'save face'
131 *Determines* terminates
136 *dock* then a word for a rabbit hutch or cage – so part of 'coney-catching' cant. Dickens made the word familiar and the metaphor dead

Thou shalt ha' my letter to mistress Amo.

DOL
Hang you—

FACE
Or madam Cæsarean.

DOL
Pox upon you, rogue,
Would I had but time to beat thee.

FACE
Subtle,
Let's know where you set up next; I'll send you
A customer, now and then, for old acquaintance:
What new course ha' you?

SUBTLE
Rogue, I'll hang myself:
That I may walk a greater devil, than thou,
And haunt thee i' the flock-bed, and the buttery.

[*Exeunt* SUBTLE, FACE, DOL]

Act V, Scene v

[*Enter*] LOVEWIT [*in Spanish costume*, PARSON]

LOVEWIT
What do you mean, my masters?

MAMMON [*without*]
Open your door,
Cheaters, bawds, conjurers.

OFFICER [*without*]
Or we'll break it open.

LOVEWIT
What warrant have you?

OFFICER
Warrant enough, sir, doubt not:
If you'll not open it.

LOVEWIT
Is there an officer, there?

OFFICER
Yes, two, or three for failing.

LOVEWIT
Have but patience,
And I will open it straight.

[*Enter* FACE]

FACE
Sir, ha' you done?
Is it a marriage? Perfect?

142 *Caesarean* Imperiall Q

141–2 *mistress Amo . . . madam Cæsarean* invented names for brothel-keepers. 'Amo' is Latin for 'I love' and 'Cæsarean' implies abortion, and perhaps, since Q has 'Imperiall', suggests a Dominatrix

145 *for* for the sake of

5 *for failing* to avoid failing

LOVEWIT Yes, my brain.

FACE

Off with your ruff, and cloak then, be yourself, sir.

SURLY [*without*]

Down with the door.

KASTRIL [*without*] 'Slight, ding it open.

LOVEWIT Hold.

Hold gentlemen, what means this violence?

[*Enter* MAMMON, SURLY, KASTRIL, ANANIAS, TRIBULATION, OFFICERS]

MAMMON

Where is this collier?

SURLY And my Captain Face?

MAMMON

These day-owls.

SURLY That are birding in men's purses.

MAMMON

Madam Suppository.

KASTRIL Doxy, my suster.

ANANIAS Locusts

Of the foul pit.

TRIBULATION Profane as Bel, and the Dragon.

ANANIAS

Worse than the grasshoppers, or the lice of Egypt.

LOVEWIT

Good gentlemen, hear me. Are you officers,
And cannot stay this violence?

OFFICER Keep the peace.

LOVEWIT

Gentlemen, what is the matter? Whom do you seek?

MAMMON

The chemical cozener.

SURLY And the Captain Pandar.

13 *suster* Q; sister F

---

9 *ding* batter, push

11 *collier* see I.i.90

12 *birding* bird-catching

13 *Madam Suppository* 'suppository' was a slang term for prostitute; perhaps also a sense of 'supposed madam' (like 'apocryphal captain')

14 *Bel, and the Dragon* two false idols in *Apocrypha*

15 *grasshoppers ... lice* two of the plagues visited upon the Egyptians (*Exodus* vii–xii)

17 *stay* prevent

KASTRIL
The nun my suster.
MAMMON Madam Rabbi.
ANANIAS Scorpions,
And caterpillars.
LOVEWIT Fewer at once, I pray you.
OFFICER
One after another, gentleman, I charge you,
By virtue of my staff—
ANANIAS They are the vessels
Of pride, lust, and the cart.
LOVEWIT Good zeal, lie still,
A little while.
TRIBULATION Peace, Deacon Ananias.
LOVEWIT
The house is mine here, and the doors are open:
If there be any such persons, as you seek for,
Use your authority, search on o' God's name.
I am but newly come to town, and finding
This tumult 'bout my door (to tell you true)
It somewhat mazed me; till my man, here, (fearing
My more displeasure) told me he had done
Somewhat an insolent part, let out my house
(Belike, presuming on my known aversion
From any air o' the town, while there was sickness)
To a Doctor, and a Captain: who, what they are,
Or where they be, he knows not.

They enter

MAMMON Are they gone?
LOVEWIT
You may go in, and search, sir. Here, I find
The empty walls, worse than I left 'em, smoked,
A few cracked pots, and glasses, and a furnace,
The ceiling filled with poesies of the candle:
And **MADAM**, with a dildo, writ o' the walls.
Only, one gentlewoman, I met here,
That is within, that said she was a widow—

24 *pride, lust, and the cart* shame, and of dishonour Q
32 *he* ed.; not in Q, F

---

20 *nun* a common irony (cf. *Hamlet*, III.i.121)
24 *and the cart* deserving of the cart
41 *poesies of the candle* stains caused by candle smoke
42 **MADAM** the typographical joke is from F
dildo artificial penis

KASTRIL
Ay, that's my suster. I'll go thump her. Where is she?
LOVEWIT
And should ha' married a Spanish Count, but he,
When he came to't, neglected her so grossly,
That I, a widower, am gone through with her.
SURLY
How! Have I lost her then?
LOVEWIT Were you the Don, sir?
Good faith, now, she does blame y'extremely, and says
You swore, and told her, you had ta'en the pains,
To dye your beard, and umbre o'er your face,
Borrowed a suit, and ruff, all for her love;
And then did nothing. What an oversight,
And want of putting forward, sir, was this!
Well fare an old harquebuzier, yet,
Could prime his powder, and give fire, and hit,
All in a twinkling.

MAMMON *comes forth*

MAMMON The whole nest are fled!
LOVEWIT
What sort of birds were they?
MAMMON A kind of choughs,
Or thievish daws, sir, that have picked my purse
Of eight score, and ten pounds, within these five weeks,
Beside my first materials; and my goods,
That lie i' the cellar: which I am glad they ha' left.
I may have home yet.
LOVEWIT Think you so, sir?
MAMMON Ay.
LOVEWIT
By order of law, sir, but not otherwise.
MAMMON
Not mine own stuff?
LOVEWIT Sir, I can take no knowledge,
That they are yours, but by public means.
If you can bring certificate, that you were gulled of 'em,
Or any formal writ, out of a court,

48 *am gone through with her* have gone through the marriage ceremony (with a suggestion of literal going through in consummation)

52 *umbre* darken

56 *harquebuzier* musketeer; armed with a harquebus (a kind of long-barrelled gun used in the army. Citizens did weapon-training drill at Mile-End Green and other open spaces. Justice Shallow reminisces about them in *2. Henry IV*, III.ii.272 ff)

That you did cozen yourself: I will not hold them.

MAMMON
I'll rather lose 'em.

LOVEWIT
That you shall not, sir,
By me, in troth. Upon these terms they are yours.
What should they ha' been, sir, turned into gold all?

MAMMON
No.
I cannot tell. It may be they should. What then?

LOVEWIT
What a great loss in hope have you sustained?

MAMMON
Not I, the commonwealth has.

FACE
Ay, he would ha' built
The city new; and made a ditch about it
Of silver, should have run with cream from Hogsden:
That, every Sunday in Moorfields, the younkers,
And tits, and tomboys should have fed on, *gratis*.

MAMMON
I will go mount a turnip cart, and preach
The end o' the world, within these two months. Surly,
What! In a dream?

SURLY
Must I needs cheat myself,
With that same foolish vice of honesty!
Come let us go, and harken out the rogues.
That Face I'll mark for mine, if e'er I meet him.

FACE
If I can hear of him, sir, I'll bring you word,
Unto your lodging: for in troth, they were strangers
To me, I thought 'em honest, as myself, sir.
[*Exeunt* MAMMON, SURLY]

They [TRIBULATION *and* ANANIAS] *come forth*

TRIBULATION
'Tis well, the Saints shall not lose all yet. Go,
And get some carts—

LOVEWIT
For what, my zealous friends?

ANANIAS
To bear away the portion of the righteous,
Out of this den of thieves.

76 *the commonwealth* Mammon has returned to his grandiloquent fantasies of philanthropy

79 *younkers* youths (especially fashionable ones)

80 *tits, and tomboys* young girls and wild girls

81 *turnip cart* a farm-wagon; the type of moveable platform employed by itinerant preachers

LOVEWIT What is that portion?
ANANIAS
The goods, sometimes the orphan's, that the Brethren,
Bought with their silver pence.
LOVEWIT What, those i' the cellar,
The knight Sir Mammon claims?
ANANIAS I do defy
The wicked Mammon, so do all the Brethren,
Thou profane man. I ask thee, with what conscience
Thou canst advance that idol, against us,
That have the seal? Were not the shillings numbered,
That made the pounds? Were not the pounds told out,
Upon the second day of the fourth week,
In the eighth month, upon the table dormant,
The year, of the last patience of the Saints,
Six hundred and ten?
LOVEWIT Mine earnest vehement botcher,
And Deacon also, I cannot dispute with you,
But, if you get you not away the sooner,
I shall confute you with a cudgel.
ANANIAS Sir.
TRIBULATION
Be patient Ananias.
ANANIAS I am strong,
And will stand up, well girt, against an host,
That threaten Gad in exile.
LOVEWIT I shall send you
To Amsterdam, to your cellar.
ANANIAS I will pray there,
Against thy house: may dogs defile thy walls,
And wasps, and hornets breed beneath thy roof,
This seat of falsehood, and this cave of cozenage.
[*Exeunt* ANANIAS, TRIBULATION]

DRUGGER *enters*

LOVEWIT
Another too?
DRUGGER Not I sir, I am no Brother.

99 *idol* Nemrod Q
116 s.d. at 118 F

---

100 *the seal Revelation* ix.4
103 *table dormant* permanent side-board
104 *of the last patience of the Saints* i.e. this is the last millenium before Doomsday
105 *botcher* see III.ii.113
111 *Gad in exile Genesis* xlix.19

LOVEWIT *He beats him away*
Away you Harry Nicholas, do you talk?
[*Exit* DRUGGER]

FACE
No, this was Abel Drugger.
To the Parson
Good sir, go,
And satisfy him; tell him, all is done:
He stayed too long a-washing of his face.
The Doctor, he shall hear of him at Westchester;
And of the Captain, tell him at Yarmouth: or
Some good port town else, lying for a wind.
[*Exit* PARSON]
If you get off the angry child, now, sir—
[*Enter* KASTRIL, DAME PLIANT]

KASTRIL *To his sister*
Come on, you ewe, you have matched most sweetly, ha' you not?
Did not I say, I would never ha' you tupped
But by a dubbed boy, to make you a lady tom?
'Slight, you are a mammet! O, I could touse you, now.
Death, mun' you marry with a pox?

LOVEWIT
You lie, boy;
As sound as you: and I am aforehand with you.

KASTRIL
Anon?

LOVEWIT
Come, will you quarrel? I will feize you, sirrah.
Why do you not buckle to your tools?

KASTRIL
God's light!
This is a fine old boy, as e'er I saw!

LOVEWIT
What, do you change your copy, now? Proceed,

124 *get* can get Q

---

117 *Harry Nicholas* Hendrick Niclaes, Anabaptist mystic and leader of 'The Family of Love'. He came to England during Edward VI's reign. In 1580 Elizabeth issued a proclamation against the sect and their publications
121 *Westchester* Chester
126 *tupped* mated (continues the farmyard talk of l.125)
127 *dubbed boy* knight
128 *mammet* doll; idiot
touse tousle; shake
129 *mun' you* must you
130 *sound* pox-free
131 *feize* do for; flog; squeeze
132 *buckle . . . tools* get on your weapons

Here stands my dove: stoop at her, if you dare.

KASTRIL
'Slight I must love him! I cannot choose, i' faith!
And I should be hanged for't. Suster, I protest,
I honour thee, for this match.

LOVEWIT
O, do you so, sir?

KASTRIL
Yes, and thou canst take tobacco, and drink, old boy,
I'll give her five hundred pound more, to her marriage,
Than her own state.

LOVEWIT
Fill a pipe-full, Jeremy.

FACE
Yes, but go in, and take it, sir.

LOVEWIT
We will.
I will be ruled by thee in anything, Jeremy.

KASTRIL
'Slight, thou art not hidebound! Thou art a Jovy boy!
Come let's in, I pray thee, and take our whiffs.

LOVEWIT
Whiff in with your sister, brother boy.
[*Exeunt* KASTRIL, DAME PLIANT]
That master
That had received such happiness by a servant,
In such a widow, and with so much wealth,
Were very ungrateful, if he would not be
A little indulgent to that servant's wit,
And help his fortune, though with some small strain
Of his own candour. Therefore, gentlemen,
And kind spectators, if I have outstripped
An old man's gravity, or strict canon, think
What a young wife, and a good brain may do:
Stretch age's truth sometimes, and crack it too.
Speak for thyself, knave.

FACE
So I will, sir. Gentlemen,
My part a little fell in this last scene,
Yet 'twas *decorum*. And though I am clean
Got off, from Subtle, Surly, Mammon, Dol,

145 *I* not in Q

---

135 *stoop* a term from falconry, appropriate to Kastril (kestrel)
144 *Jovy boy* jovial fellow
145 *whiffs* smokes
152 *candour* whiteness of soul
154 *canon* regularity
159 *decorum* the classical principle of consistency and fittingness

Hot Ananias, Dapper, Drugger, all
With whom I traded; yet I put myself
On you, that are my country: and this pelf,
Which I have got, if you do quit me, rests
To feast you often, and invite new guests.

THE END

pelf: stolen property

163 *my country* my jury (chosen from the neighbourhood)
164 *quit* acquit

This Comoedie vvas first acted, in the yeere 1610.

By the Kings Maiesties SERVANTS.

The principall Comœdians were,

RIC. BVRBADGE.	IOH. HEMINGS.
IOH. LOWIN.	WILL. OSTLER.
HEN. CONDEL.	IOH. VNDERWOOD.
ALEX. COOKE.	NIC. TOOLY.
ROB. ARMIN.	WILL. EGLESTONE.

With the allowance of the Master of REVELLS.

Cast list which appears as the final page of the play in the 1616 edition of Jonson's *Works* (British Library G.11630, f. 678).